How to survive and succeed as a **headteacher**

Kevin Harcombe

Dedication

To my family – Kerry, Caitlin, Patrick and Bridie – who helped me to survive and succeed as a headteacher

How to survive and succeed as a headteacher
106646
ISBN-13: 978 1 85503 487 7

First published 2010
Reprinted 2010, 2011, 2012, 2013

Printed in the UK for LDA
LDA, Findel Education, Hyde Buildings, Ashton Road, Hyde, Cheshire, SK14 4SH

Contents

Contents

Introduction

Why be a headteacher?

If you ask a class of school-age children 'What do you want to be when you grow up?', you will get the usual footballer / supermodel / pop star answers from the optimistic ones, and maybe hairdresser / vet / bus driver from the rest. If the school is in the leafy suburbs you may get someone wanting to be an actuary or a picture restorer.

Headteacher, anyone?

Everyone remembers a good headteacher. It is one of the best jobs in the world.

You have a pivotal influence on the future opportunities for all the children who are educated in your school. You are helping to create the next generation, enabling them to shape their values, taking part in their life's journey and leading them by the hand for at least part of the way. Everyone remembers a good headteacher. It is one of the best jobs in the world. You don't get to score a last-minute winner in the Champions League Final or strut down a catwalk to a thousand flashbulbs, but you have other kinds of reward.

No one ever said it was an easy or lucrative job. Improving a school – for that's mainly what a headteacher does – is hard work, made harder by things like Ofsted, league tables and seemingly endless initiatives. But if a cold front of cumulo-nimbus is spoiling your blue-sky thinking or if, when urged to think outside the box, you have difficulty remembering where you left it, don't be put off – it could still be the job for you. If you are in it already and are feeling a bit lost or dispirited, take heart, help is at hand.

Chapter 1
It's all about the children, stupid!

In Bill Clinton's first presidential election campaign there were posters at campaign HQ reading simply 'It's the economy, stupid.' That was advice never to lose focus on the fact that elections are won and lost on the ability to run the economy.

For a headteacher, the message is 'It's the children, stupid!'

For a headteacher, the message is 'It's the children, stupid!' And that's not just about equipping them with basic skills, but about shaping their attitudes and encouraging them to have dreams and ambitions.

With all the extraneous stuff that lands on a headteacher's desk, it's easy to lose sight of what you are there for: to help children learn and grow, and to help them 'dare to dream'. The building works, the blocked toilets, the latest government or LA strategy, the requests from IT providers, the PTA's desire to have yet another non-uniform day, the mail shots from myriad consultants and travelling players – they should all be subjected to one simple test: how will this help the children's learning? If the answer is 'It won't' or 'I don't know', then ditch them.

That doesn't mean you can ditch statutory initiatives, much as you might like to. You have to be a bit Machiavellian in the children's interests (see Chapter 9). It does mean that you have to be ruthless and decisive in deciding what you will spend your budget on and, equally importantly, your time (and others' time) on. Some decisions require a little lateral thinking. For instance, hosting trainee teachers has a cost: staff have to support them and attend meetings with the college tutor, and you may see a fall in the children's quality of work when they are taught by a novice. All this may lead to parental complaints that affect your time and the image of your school. Conversely, staff develop through supporting trainees and it's good to put it on their CV, the children's work may maintain its quality or – not beyond the realms of possibility – improve and parents will be delighted. It may free up the class teacher to do some small-group work or have some additional monitoring and support time (MAST). All of that has a positive effect on the school's ability to help their children learn – which is and should remain your core business.

So much to do

Scan through your diary and/or school improvement plan (SIP). Make a list of all the tasks that have to be done in the next term. It is probably dauntingly long, but as you tick off each successfully completed task you will see that, on what sometimes seems like a mountain, you have left the foothills behind and have the summit in sight.

When you get that 'What am I actually achieving' feeling – often on a Monday morning or following a difficult meeting – take time out to make a list of what you have already achieved. Invariably you will find it is satisfyingly long. Take a few moments to pat yourself on the back and congratulate staff and children – then face the challenge, reinvigorated and refreshed by your own capability.

Managing the paper

When drowning in a sea of paper, try the following system:

1. Set up a series of files labelled by date for the current month, by subsequent months, and 'Today' and 'Tomorrow'.
2. As the paper and emails arrive, file them according to when they need to be dealt with.
3. You or your secretary transfer the work to the 'Today' and 'Tomorrow' files when their date approaches.
4. It also helps to have a 'To do next year' page in your diary so you can record notes for action/appointments/ events outside the current year.

Improving schools is hard graft

It is no surprise to me that many, though not all, education consultants – the snake-oil salesmen and smoke-and-mirrors merchants – do so well out of schools. Rather like alternative medicine, they provide quick fixes or a glimmer of hope when conventional remedies are failing. When faced with very low attainment and with the LA or Ofsted breathing down your neck, it is tempting to try something different: revamp the curriculum along innovative lines based on best practice in Finland, maybe, or introduce Indian head massage in Year 3. It's different, it's daring, and it defies the perceived drive to narrow the curriculum. Oh, and it generally doesn't work. There's another 'd' to bear in mind: it's a displacement activity.

Stop deceiving yourself. Primary education is all about helping children learn and grow, which means – without wanting to seem reductionist about things – that by the time they leave you they can read, write and do number well enough to carry on learning at the next stage. 'How Gradgrindian, how narrow, how devoid of joy that is for the poor children', I hear some colleagues protest. But how devoid of joy is it for Ahmed or Isobel to arrive at the next school two years behind in reading, unable to say or write a complex sentence and not knowing multiplication facts? They can paint, they can devise a rap, they can jive! Those achievements will count for nothing if they leave school with no GCSEs because they weren't given basic skills in KS1 and 2.

This does not mean that I advocate a narrow or utilitarian curriculum, quite the reverse. It's not either/or. It's and! You don't have to spend every minute in school teaching writing, reading and how to do sums. Art and music and sport and the humanities and the rest are all vital, only – and this may be heresy, I know – not as vital as reading and writing. There needs to be balance and trade-offs, and the balance needs to be tipped towards ensuring basic skills are mastered. It's not rap or read. It's not sport or spelling. It's rap and read, sport and spelling.

Make acquiring the basic skills a mission that is undertaken with dedication, excitement and enjoyment.

It's hard graft. Accept it. Embrace it. Make acquiring the basic skills a mission that is undertaken with dedication, excitement and enjoyment. It's hard, but it never has to be dull – it must never be dull. If a child is painting, do they have the opportunity to talk about the painting to improve speaking and listening? Does someone write and read out a report on football or netball matches? Can children work out their running speed over a 100-metre route they have measured themselves? That's simple cross-curricular stuff, but it all reinforces language and mathematical skills. Is the quality of writing the children achieve in English transferred and maintained when writing in RE or history? Are science lessons or geography-themed studies opportunities to incorporate practical mathematics? However you structure your curriculum, language skills in particular can be developed through everything else.

Have you ever heard teachers say 'If it wasn't for the children this job would be great!'? If they say that seriously, they do not deserve to work in school. Children are the job. If the children in your setting are polite, hard working, conscientious and guaranteed straight 5s in the SATs, lucky you! (I bet their parents are demanding, though, which brings its own trials.) If your children are rough, slackers and seemingly unlikely to get anywhere near a level 4 in anything, that's a challenge – but never an insurmountable one. You can only work with the children you've got and that's what you get your salary for. If, to paraphrase Oscar Wilde, you and your school are 'in the gutter', it is most important that you are looking up at the stars.

It is not complicated. What needs to be done is fairly straightforward and set out in this book. Making sure it is done is the hard bit. It requires determination. It tends to be the human bit that's toughest to do because we all want to be liked, and giving out true but unpleasant messages won't win us any popularity contests. But think of the children!

Chapter 2
Vision

In medieval times some poor souls were burnt at the stake because they had visions. Now leaders are hung out to dry if they don't have one. A lot of claptrap has been talked and written about vision … so let me help you cope with the pile.

At a meeting of staff and governors, ask the simple question 'What is it we want to achieve here?' People will often be most passionate about what they don't want to see, so stipulate that all responses are to be framed in a positive way. You'll get a variety of answers: good behaviour, good SATs results, happy children, and so on. They are all noble, even essential, aims, but what is the driving force that underpins them?

If you're the quiet, self-effacing type like me, you may be diffident about promoting your vision. It's a bit personal and passionate, isn't it? To help you formulate your own vision, here are a few key questions:

- What are the values that you think should be passed on to those who will be the citizens of tomorrow's world?
- Keep it simple. Ask yourself 'What kind of school do I want to be head of?'
- Keep it clear. Avoid jargon and the poetic language that some vision statements are written in. This is not Star Trek. You are not boldly going into the farthest reaches of the galaxy. If no one knows what you mean, how can they put it into practice?
- Keep it explicit. Every time a new initiative arrives in your Inbox or lands with a thump on your desk (initiatives never come in slim volumes), ask yourself 'Will this help achieve my vision or get in the way of it?' If the answer is 'Get in the way', be brave and consign it to the bin.
- Keep it brief. It's not an Oscar acceptance speech, nor should it be a litany of everything you want to achieve.

Google's vision is to 'organize the world's information and make it universally accessible and useful'. The task is huge and ambitious but clear, simple and explicit.

Microsoft's vision is 'to help people and businesses throughout the world realize their full potential', which is huge and vague.

Here's a school vision that is brief, simple, explicit and clear.

Our vision is to provide a happy, caring and stimulating environment where children will recognise and achieve their full potential through carefully planned teaching and learning as measured through year-on-year progress, so that they can make their best contribution to society.

Whether you have a vision, or had one and mislaid it, or don't think it's up to scratch, the following activity may help you.

Activity 2.1: Vision

Ask groups of 3 or 4 to imagine the school as you would like it to be five years in the future.

In no more than 50 words, get each group to describe what the school is like at that time and what your role in it is.

Alternatively draw it, clearly showing where you are and what your role is.

Fix each statement/picture on a wall. Groups visit them. The groups that devised each talk to the other groups about it for two minutes.

Discuss the common elements of the future thinking. Each group then tries to combine these in a statement of no more than 50 words.

From this activity a range of themes will quickly emerge that embody the values which will underpin the school's vision. Write it up and see if it lives up to these criteria: is it simple, clear, explicit and brief?

The media – a double-edged sword

For the good times ...

It's worth taking a look at an important aspect of your role before you go any further. How good are you at celebrating and publicising good news? Do you keep a folder of thank-you letters at the school entrance that parents can read? Are there lots of photographs of the great work you do plastered round your school and in your website and newsletters? Be proud of every success. Photos in the local press do more good than harm.

Be very wary of trusting the press. 'I can put a good angle on this if only you would give me all the details', might be one plea. 'You can speak off the record' might be another. Don't. If you tell a reporter something off the record, ten minutes later a colleague of theirs will ring and say, 'I've heard ... Would you like to confirm or deny this report?' They've got you.

A resolute and consistent 'No comment' will deal with most cases. If your LA has a press office, refer all details to them and let them handle it. Get your own version of events out to parents by newsletter or email or website, remembering that the press can access such material and may quote it out of context.

Chapter 3
Building the team

You've got the job and you are sitting in your office wondering what to do now. You may be particularly daunted about attending meetings with experienced and established headteachers. If you have a headteacher mentor, ask if you can walk in alongside them. If not, remember that experienced heads will still make mistakes and sometimes feel daunted themselves. High achievers are not perfect. You'll soon find there are things you know and can do that they don't and can't. Through collaboration and networking, headteachers and schools can learn a lot from each other. I found in my early days that if I telephoned a head for advice, they were always generous with it. Make sure that when someone rings you, you are equally generous.

Some mornings you may think 'This is a grown-up's job and I feel only 14 years old! Who was mad enough to appoint me?' Well, it was a panel of sensible people (who generally know what they're doing). As there's no one else; it's up to you.

Good news: other people are the means through which you can achieve most.
Bad news: other people can stop you achieving anything at all.

In 25 years of teaching I have learned two things (a slightly disappointing tally): life can always be better, and teaching and learning can always be better. Change is always with us – stand still for a moment and you are going backwards.

First, take a moment to ponder your staff list – all staff, not just teachers. Assistants and support staff are key players too. Do you know who's good at what? Are you spreading their expertise? You work with and through people – and, if need be, round them. Persuade, negotiate, remind, catch good practice and celebrate it.

Some people do such a fantastic job that you miss them only when they've gone. You'll soon notice if your caretaker/cleaner decamps because things will quickly become dusty and dirty, and you will be the one locking up and moaning about the state of the floor in Class 9. You'd notice if the admin officer or bursar won the lottery and retired because of the queue outside your office every day to buy uniform / check when term ends and do the million other things coped with efficiently by this member of the team.

Teaching old dogs new tricks

When you take over a school, you inherit the previous incumbent's staff and a lot of interpersonal baggage. Staff will be curious, if not downright anxious,

about what you are going to do. This effect is magnified if they regard your predecessor as an educational titan and you as a here today, gone tomorrow (hopefully), minnow. At first sight you may not be impressed by the staff team, comparing them unfavourably with the one you left behind. Find out what their strengths are and arrange them to play to those strengths. March with the army you have.

Consider your immediate team (staff and governors) and your extended team (children, parents and wider community). Some of those have been at the school long enough to have laid the foundation stone. Get the motivation and training right and make the most of what they have to offer, rather than assigning them a role to which they are completely unsuited. An audit of strengths and weaknesses would be a useful starting point.

Have a long, hard look at the leadership team you have inherited. You must establish your credibility with them quickly, and there may be some scepticism about your capabilities. One of them may have applied for your post. Are they up for the work you want them to do? You could use the Leadership Team Audit (p. 12). Itemise the qualities you want in your leadership team and match these to the qualities the existing team have. Can the gaps be addressed by training? Can you use any bonuses? You may have a deputy who is National Professional Qualification for Headship (NPQH) qualified or a lead teacher in some aspect of learning.

Leadership team audit

Name ________________________ Role ________________________

Never ________________________ Always

Do you contribute significantly to policy and practice?	________________________
Do you promote collective responsibility for their implementation?	________________________
Do you contribute to the professional development of colleagues by coaching, mentoring and providing effective feedback?	________________________
Are you able to access, analyse and interpret information, including data?	________________________
Do you challenge, motivate and influence others to achieve high goals?	________________________
Do you maintain effective relationships with colleagues and the wider school community?	________________________
Do you collaborate and network with others beyond the school?	________________________
Does your performance improve and develop year on year?	________________________
Do you model the principles and practice of effective teaching and learning across the school?	________________________
Do you model the values and vision of the school?	________________________

Place a mark along each line according to your self-assessment. Prior to your personal interview you need to give consideration to how you do the things above, and have some concrete examples.

Model flexible leadership yourself, aiming to reach the point where you are strategic director and the minutiae are undertaken by others. The only thing a person needs to be a leader is the opportunity to lead.

How not to build a team

When Brian Clough, the late football manager, took over from Don Revie, he axed and set fire to his highly regarded predecessor's office desk. He told the team to throw away their winner's medals because they had obtained them by cheating. That was not motivational. Clough was unsuccessful at Leeds United.

How do you make sure your people are on your side? Start small but think big. Establish trust early on. Tell the staff your first days and weeks will be spent finding out about them, how they work and how effectively the school functions. Research shows that successful schools are predicated on building trust to establish collaborative strength. Getting the atmosphere right is important.

You will never find a member of staff unwilling to comment on their headteacher. What they will talk about is not what you say but what you do. What you model is what makes the greatest impression – negative as well as positive.

A study of 13 successful primary schools, covering a wide range of social advantage and disadvantage, identified these among their distinguishing characteristics:

- Collegiality and collaboration
- Building trust
- Valuing people
- Identifying key players
- Successful recruiting
- Making the most of staff meetings
- Dealings with staff
- Working with governors
- Relating to parents
- Developing the children.

Collegiality and collaboration

How Very Effective Primary Schools Work, by C.R. James, T. Elliott, M. Connolly and G. Dunning (2006). Paul Chapman Publishing, London.

There was extensive and intensive joint working, a high level of trust and a powerful sense of mutual accountability. Everyone was required to be a team player and to conform.

Conformity means that within the school, variation – major differences in quality of practice between classes – is minimised. Collegiality and collaboration magnify the power of individuals so they are greater than the sum of their parts.

Building trust

Don't try to rush the trust-building process. You may have been to INSET where a drama inspector encouraged people to fall backwards off tables into the arms of colleagues to learn trust. Some exercises involve people sharing personal stories or revealing their personality type, based on the notion that shared vulnerability can be the beginning of trust. The process can't be rushed and revealing vulnerability may make you *more* vulnerable. Why not build up trust and credibility simply by listening and being open and honest?

Building trust – some essentials

1. Be explicit about your core values and vision – if people know where you are going (and why), they are more likely to join you. Unity of purpose is key to school improvement. Remember that if an intransigent staff member doesn't like your vision or core values, they are free to leave at any time.
2. Do what you say you will do. Inconsistency and failure to deliver on promises undermine trust and credibility.
3. Clear and frequent communication is the best antidote to rumours and misconceptions. It could be face to face (best), through a senior teacher (nearly as good), by notices on the staffroom whiteboard (just OK) or email (not recommended). Always read back an email on a sensitive or contentious subject to yourself and add the words 'you bastard' to each sentence – that's how it may be read by the recipient.
4. Encourage wide involvement in decision-making. What do others think? Be clear that you are consulting, not abdicating responsibility or offering a vote – unless you are offering a vote. The final responsibility lies with you. Seek others' opinions; only idiots and despots believe they have all the answers. There is a huge amount of expertise in any school, but never be so concerned to hear everyone's views that you procrastinate – staff will wish you would make the decision because they've important things to be getting on with.
5. Make sure that staff know your door is always open and you want to hear their views and ideas. Walking down the corridor to the head's office can be daunting. One teacher once told me 'You've no idea how hard it is to come and speak to you in your office.' I thought I was an approachable person, but she quaked every time she came to my room. I was able to reassure her, and she now often comes with sensible and useful suggestions.

Valuing people

There is a story about President John F. Kennedy visiting the NASA Space Center. Escaping the official tour, he went into the typing pool and asked a secretary, 'What is your job here?' She replied, 'I'm helping to put a man on the moon.' She felt both valued and motivated, and was absolutely focused. How many of your staff would say in response to that question, 'I'm helping to shape the next generation'?

If you show you value people, they are more likely to value others. Eventually this will permeate the whole school and will have a salutary effect on the children.

Get round to see everyone – cleaner, secretaries, deputy – at the start of the day, even if just to say 'Good morning'. You can tell a lot about the well-being of your team this way. If you ask 'How are you?', be prepared for some frank responses.

Always remember to say 'Thank you' – 'Please' and 'Thank you' go a long way. After a late parents' meeting, a simple thank you on their noticeboard will remind staff that they're not taken for granted.

Smile – the best advice to new teachers is to remind them to smile at the children, and heads should remember to smile at their team. (There are exceptions – when administering a dressing-down grinning makes you look malicious.)

Value people with specific praise: 'Your comment to the meeting was really helpful'; 'Your room looks so welcoming to the children.'

The leader's mood and behaviours drive the moods and behaviours of everyone else. A cranky and ruthless boss creates a toxic organisation filled with underachievers who ignore opportunities: an inspirational, inclusive leader spawns acolytes for whom any challenge is surmountable.

D. Goleman, *The New Leaders* (2002)

Separate the personal from the professional. As a new teacher I was once told by the admin officer 'Avoid the head before 11 o'clock. He's grouchy in the morning.' That is poor leadership and deeply unprofessional. You may have had a bad night, or be poorly or generally grumpy, but you should not take it out on your staff.

Some staff are easy to value. When they walk in, you smile, your spirits soar, your heart beats a little faster and you think 'Here comes so-and-so – everything will be fine!'

There are the ones who are not so easy too. Short of introducing an award for not whingeing for a week, how do you cope with them? Most schools have at least one curmudgeon or well-poisoner. Some have a staffroom full. They've seen it all before. They didn't like it the first time, second time round it irritates the hell out of them. They've had more headteachers than an NAHT conference and most of those resigned or vanished mysteriously. Your options are limited, as follows:

- Woo them with your charm and vision. (All right, unlikely.)
- Accept they'll never be your greatest fans but as long as they do a competent, professional job you can live with them. You're not judged on being liked.
- Keep leaving the vacancy list in their in-tray. (Joke – this is good practice for someone coming to the end of a temporary contract, but for someone permanent it could be construed as constructive dismissal.)
- Have a full and frank discussion with them. Say you hope they will wholeheartedly embrace your policies and practices. If they don't you will be familiarising yourself with the disciplinary procedures, and if they simply can't you will be familiarising yourself with the support/capability procedures. Clarity is a wonderful thing. Resignations may follow, but hopefully not yours.

Let's assume, though, that your staff are pleasant and willing and keen to move forward. What now?

Identifying the key players

These may be existing senior teachers. There may be new teachers who are hungry for advancement and training who could be part of the drive to move the school forward too.

Interview all staff within the first fortnight. Ask them what they think works currently and what needs fixing. Usually, but not always, if it ain't broke don't fix it.

Sometimes a problem that looms like a rain cloud on Monday morning will have solved itself by Tuesday afternoon. Sometimes a wait-and-see approach saves time and effort and avoids making a problem worse.

In the first two to three weeks you are looking and learning. This is not a time for rushed-through, blood-on-the-carpet reforms.

'Happy workers don't get sick' goes the saying. Try telling that to a teacher who has spent the last lesson avoiding the sneezing of children coming down with the latest disease. There is a kernel of truth in it, however. Stressed and unhappy staff are likely to succumb to infection. They are also more likely to offer a doctor's note identifying stress or anxiety as their reason for absence, a wake-up call if it happens to more than one member of staff. (An individual you are supporting or pursuing under capability or disciplinary guidelines will often go sick.)

Sometimes it is enlightening to map out when staff absences occur – if it is regularly round a birthday, or the same week in February, it will be worth investigating. Be careful how you pursue such cases as unions will leap on you if you are seen to be victimising a teacher. Get your facts straight, and be cautious about using covert surveillance methods (parking down their street to see if they nip out when they should be working), which are subject to strict regulation.

Once you've built a team, don't work it to death. Staff meetings should start and end on time – or preferably earlier. If there is no need for a meeting, don't hold one – instead give it over to staff well-being and send everyone home at 3.30 p.m.

Absences reaching, say, 15 days in any 12-month period might warrant an informal interview along the lines of 'How are you feeling?' or more formally a referral to Occupational Health, if your LA has such a department.

Team-building

You have inherited a leadership team who have never been trained – or allowed – to lead. One is on the verge of retirement and is clearly coasting. The other lacks initiative.

The soon to retire: Following the audit (Activity 2.1, p. 12), identify perceived strengths and weaknesses. Confirm these by interview and observation. The simple idea is to make maximum use of the skills they have and address any deficiencies through training – much of which you may be able to do in house, quickly. Set out your expectations clearly and do some confidence-building: 'You have skills that haven't been called upon. I can help you make use of them. You have 30+ years of experience at high level and this school needs that. This is how I see your role in the remaining year of your career. It's a chance for you to go out on a high!' This person is drawing a salary for carrying out a leadership role. You need to try and get value for money, recognising that with a year to go motivation might be a problem.

The initiative-free leader: After the audit and interview, you will have a better idea of why this person lacks initiative. Have they never been allowed to use it? Do they lack ability or confidence? Find out what training they have had in the past two years and what they have done as a result. This person needs time to talk about and reflect on what leadership entails. Try setting up a small project in which they report back at the end, without checking every step. Tell them: 'It seems that you are very efficient at carrying out other people's plans but you always keep checking back with me. I want you to work autonomously, within the vision we have set for the school.'

Sometimes you can't get the wrong people out of the tent, so you have to get the right people inside. That is why recruitment is such an important aspect of what leaders do. It may be easy and comfortable to settle for good rather than outstanding. I had a goodish teacher who was coming to the end of a temporary contract. Because there were lots of other pressures on at the time, I talked to my assistant head about rolling the contract forward and making it permanent – it was easier and would be good enough. She upbraided me: 'You taught me never to settle for anything but the best and I don't think we should settle now.' I had developed her as a leader and she was coming back to prick my conscience, giving me the steel to have the difficult conversation in which I told that teacher the contract would not be renewed.

Successful recruiting

It is difficult to motivate cynical or ill-disciplined people. It is better to recruit the self-motivated and self-disciplined – those who wake up every day determined to do the best they can do and be the best they can be.

Talent spot new teachers

A vacancy is one of the most exciting opportunities in the life of a headteacher. Even if you have lost a superbly talented, experienced and expert staff member, there is a buzz about how you plug the gap and move forward. If an assistant head is promoted to another school, do you seek a replacement from within or without? Do you restructure using teaching and learning responsibilities (TLR) posts, or employ a newly qualified teacher to balance your salary budget and bring fresh blood, fresh thinking and fresh possibilities to the school?

Frame the advert

Some adverts are designed to attract dull people. Here's one: 'New teacher wanted for Year-4 class. Interest in geography would be advantageous. Please send sae for application pack.' Your advert must attract the most vibrant, sparkling brains the teaching world has to offer. It needs to excite, promise, and have the *crème de la crème* beating a path to your door.

We are 30 delightful and occasionally delirious Year-4 children who are looking for a kind, smiling and clever teacher to excite us and help us learn. Our school is a happy and fun place to work and our head says you'll get the best training you've ever had. (He also said he'll work you hard but we're not sure if we should mention that.) Also, we've peeked in the staffroom and they have cakes!

Please visit us and collect an application form, or you can find out about us from our website, download an application form there and return it by email.

Of course, children should be involved – not necessarily at short listing but as part of the tasks and interviewing process. They make the same choice as

the adult panel nine times out of ten. Children's involvement in questioning the candidate is important. They should come up with their own questions – it will be obvious to candidates if they are mouthing ones prepared for them by a teacher, and you want to show off your pupil-voice practice. This method led at a recent interview to one child asking candidates 'Do you know how to calculate the running speed of a zebra?' When a candidate replied in the negative, the child consoled them with 'Don't worry, none of the others could either.'

Make the job attractive. That might not mean more cash. For example, you are looking for a newly qualified teacher (NQT) and want the very best, but yours is a struggling school, with a just satisfactory Ofsted, in a deprived area, with potentially unruly children and a staffroom full of complacency. How do you make the brightest and best graduates go for that? It starts with a good advert.

Can you cut the mustard in a challenging school?

For September, we want the best graduate possible to come and make a difference to our children. We can offer you long hours and hard work. We can offer children who need you and your skills – but they don't know it. We can offer you the usual starting salary and also a supportive team and access to regular leadership development seminars with the Head and leadership team to develop leadership capabilities and get your career off to a flying start. We can also offer you the indisputable bonus of an exciting place to work in and the chance to say later in your career 'I was at the start of turning that school round' to admiring looks from your colleagues and girls/boys on the beach.

Selection will be rigorous. We are looking for first-class and upper-second-class honours degrees and top references. Some of you will apply and won't get an interview because we know there are hundreds of self-motivated, self-disciplined graduates out there who will want to be part of this mission. We promise you an exhilarating and exhausting experience. If you think you can cut it, further details may be obtained from ...

The advert above is honest. It will appeal to those with a sense of mission and also to a sense of competition: can they get this job? Once you have the recruit you want, next time there is a vacancy you can use the experience of that recruit as a lever to attract similar quality applicants. You build results gradually. You slowly build reputation. Those results and reputation will attract more supportive parents and better-quality staff, so the success snowballs until yours is one of the most sought-after schools in your area. All you have to do then is keep it like that.

Interviews

I like to have a variety of expertise on interview panels: a governor, myself, a teacher from the year group where the vacancy is and possibly another senior teacher. Questions will vary according to the post. I like an informal approach that lets us see what the candidate knows rather than what they don't know. In particular, the extent of their emotional intelligence is usually key for me. I've seen fantastically qualified applicants who lack both empathy and common sense – they didn't get the job. I always see teachers teach – usually two of us will observe a half-hour lesson – and generally ask them to teach to their perceived strengths rather than being prescriptive. For senior appointments I include a data-analysis exercise and an in-tray task. I currently include children who question the applicants, mainly to see how they respond to what can be quite challenging questions. The discussion about whom to appoint is based around the person specification we draw up and is collegiate – everyone's opinion counts – but not necessarily democratic. There is no counting of votes.

Four years ago I made the error of delegating the lesson observation section to two senior staff. When it came to decision time, they were adamant that one candidate who had, they said, taught a fantastic lesson but given a so-so interview should get the job. I wanted another candidate. There was a free and frank exchange of views and I regretted not having seen this great lesson as the interview showing had been poor. I went along with my senior staff, but added grumpily, 'If this appointment goes wrong it'll be you putting it right.' They were right, I was wrong. The teacher we appointed as NQT is now my assistant head. The moral of the story is this: always see every part of the selection process and always listen and act on the advice of trusted senior staff.

Making the most of staff meetings

Staff meetings are an opportunity to communicate the latest initiatives and keep tabs on how the school is performing on a daily basis.

This is an art that comes with experience. These thoughts will ensure you make the most of them:

- Staff meetings are an opportunity to communicate the latest initiatives and keep tabs on how the school is performing on a daily basis.
- They are a great form of INSET, and need to be planned in advance. At the start of each year I provide staff with a blank calendar and ask them to pencil in the staff meetings they will need for their particular subject/aspect.
- With the senior leadership team (SLT), I ensure the priorities on the SIP are balanced, and make sure I leave one meeting a term free for work–life balance (go home early) and some others blank in report-writing season or to deal with unforeseen issues.
- Do make the setting fairly formal. Don't hold them in the staffroom – comfy chairs and coffee and cakes are not conducive to business-like meetings.
- Host each one in a different classroom, giving all staff a chance to see each other's working environment, displays and layouts. The first couple of minutes can be given over to the host teacher to explain how the room works. Other staff can then make constructive suggestions about how the room might be improved for learning.
- Start and finish promptly. Never have meetings that last more than an hour – it's the end of the working day and people are tired. If the business of the meeting finishes early, close the meeting early – don't spin it out to stamp your authority on the staff.
- If there is nothing to discuss, cancel the meeting but give the cancellation a purpose for the time saved, calling it 'additional reflection time', for instance.
- If you are doing group activities, make sure you mix the groups to avoid cliques.

Staff-meeting characters

The cynic: Has been there, done it, worn the T-shirt and sold it on eBay. May be quiet and irritating, with a smug smile that says 'This is nothing new, we did this years ago before the last head made us do something different.' Deal with this by using openings such as 'One or two of you may think this has been done before but it's different in these respects ...'.

The whinger: Life, apparently, owes them a living – they don't want to work for it. This sort of teacher complains they are six minutes short of their PPA entitlement accumulated over the past term. Most likely to say 'Not more initiatives – when are we going to fit this in?' Never allow rabble-rousing by rising to the bait – make a statement along the lines of 'I'm more than happy to discuss this with you after the meeting, but we need to finish on time tonight so I don't eat in to your hard-pressed time.' This sounds reasonably well even said through gritted teeth.

The rabbit in headlights: Totally fazed by whatever you're suggesting. Most likely to say nothing – too terrified to speak. Deal with by smiling encouragingly and talking to them quietly afterwards to make sure all is well.

The low-level disrupter: Passes round toffees / holiday snaps. Most likely to say: 'Tic tac, anyone?' Deal with by eating the entire box of tic tacs.

The majority of staff will be quietly or vocally supportive and will often help you deal with these characters – but only if you've built your alliances carefully.

Make SLT meetings open to all staff. Few of the rest will attend often or at all, but open access is important and gives aspiring leaders a chance to see how these meetings run.

Senior leadership team meetings

- Make SLT meetings open to all staff. Few of the rest will attend often or at all, but open access is important and gives aspiring leaders a chance to see how these meetings run.
- An agenda is not always essential. Sometimes you will be simply discussing the process of the SIP.
- Some schools formally include a governor or CA or bursar on their SLT or invite them to specific meetings.

Dealings with staff

Establishing credibility

You have to gain the confidence of your staff. Some will be anxious, especially if the previous incumbent was concerned about their quality.

You have to gain the confidence of your staff. Some will be anxious, especially if the previous incumbent was concerned about their quality. They may be anxious about you changing things they think don't need changing. Some will be excited – you are the new broom they've been waiting for. You need to manage their expectations too. Some will be suspicious of you and what you intend to do. Some will be blasé and just get on with life. You need to get a message across that covers all the bases. In most cases that message will go something like this:

I'm so pleased to be head of this school. I'm looking forward to learning from each of you how the school currently operates and what we might do together to take it forward. For the first few weeks I'll probably be walking round with a slightly bewildered look on my face, pushing doors clearly marked 'Pull'. I'll be finding out what the school's like. I shall be in and out of classrooms – no clipboard, formal lesson observation won't start just yet – to see you and your children. I'll also be talking to each of you individually to find out what you currently do and what your ideas are for taking this school forward.

Your tone needs to combine reassurance together with your commitment to valuing everyone, at the same time leaving little doubt that the buck stops with you.

Your tone needs to combine reassurance together with your commitment to valuing everyone, at the same time leaving little doubt that the buck stops with you.

Try not to make notes as you go round – nip back to your office for that. Remember that although you've said you'll just be looking, if something illegal or dangerous is going on you will have to sort it out. One of the commonest reasons for failing an Ofsted is the lack of Standard Operating Procedures (SOPs; some schools call it policy guidance) – simple things that should be done consistently. You may have a SOP for dealing with disruptive pupils – say, sending a child to fetch an assistant or teacher. In schools without or not following SOPs, you may see children who have been disruptive and chucked out of class wandering about. SOPs are most likely to fail when supply staff who have not been properly briefed are employed.

In your initial interviews with staff, keep the questions simple. How would you describe your current role? What is the best thing about the school? What really needs improvement? What part could you play in that? You need to ensure individual confidentiality and anonymity, and to collate the results and feed them back to staff and governors.

If at the end of the exercise you are feeling a trifle daunted, do your SWOT analysis – identifying Strengths, Weaknesses, Opportunities and Threats. That may make you feel as though you're starting to put things to rights.

Team-building activities

Some people swear by these. Others swear if they have to do them. Paintballing, anyone? Crewing a sailing ship to the Isle of Wight? I prefer a drink and a pub meal, or chicken in a basket down at the greyhound track. Ask the team, of course, as they'll have their own ideas. Remember that some decisions have to be executive ones.

Underperforming staff

You may make mistakes in recruitment. You need to identify that early so you can take early action to rectify it quickly. Sometimes a member of the team will get it wrong, lose motivation or do something unprofessional. Show understanding, but be explicit about your expectations. These are hard messages for a staff member to hear, and they may be hard to give. Getting the hard messages across is a determining factor in ensuring your school continues to improve and operate with your vision at its forefront.

Students with the best teachers in the best schools learn at least three times more each year than those with the worst teachers in the worst schools.

Students with the best teachers in the best schools learn at least three times more each year than those with the worst teachers in the worst schools. That is one reason why when secondary students look at their new timetables they don't ask 'Which subjects have I got?' but 'Which teachers will I have this year?'

Giving hard messages to staff – top tips

1 Giving hard messages can be stressful. Make sure you have your facts straight beforehand. Rehearse what you are going to say. Have notes to ensure you cover everything.
2 Give hard messages quickly – get your bad news out clearly, unequivocally and dispassionately. Don't chat for half an hour, then mumble a sentence about how poor a lesson was as they are leaving.
3 Give hard messages promptly, at the earliest opportunity, if you are sure of your ground. Don't add to your stress by stewing something over a night or a weekend.
4 Separate the personal from the professional. An underperforming teacher may be delightful as a neighbour; they may organise brilliant staff nights out, but they are paid to do a professional job and children's futures depend on your making sure they do it.
5 With messages relating to overall capability or disciplinary matters always seek advice from HR first, and have a third person at the meeting to make notes. The staff member should be told in writing that they are encouraged to be accompanied to the meeting by a representative of their professional association or a colleague.

Supporting weak teachers

You support a weak teacher because you believe they can improve and you want them to improve. Often, though by no means always, they will want to improve. Your aim is to raise every teacher to the level of the best teacher in your school.

The first way to support teachers is by monitoring and evaluating their work and giving them clear, detailed and honest feedback. That is your duty as head, and it is each teacher's right to be developed professionally. Make the feedback honest even if it contravenes the rule of thumb of two positives to each negative. Once you have identified areas of strength and weakness you need to address them. If there is a weakness in questioning or behaviour management, for example, you can release them to see a teacher in action who is especially strong in the areas. You then debrief them – what did they learn from their visit? Form a judgement about whether what they've learned is what you intended. Support them in incorporating what they have learned into their daily practice. Next time you observe them – you will be observing them frequently

– if they have succeeded the case is closed. Keep a watching brief to ensure improvements are sustained.

One of the commonest and most frustrating scenarios is a teacher improving sufficiently to come off informal or formal support only to slip back a couple of weeks, months or even days later.

One of the commonest and most frustrating scenarios is a teacher improving sufficiently to come off informal or formal support only to slip back a couple of weeks, months or even days later. You have to start again. Ratchet up the support and pressure if this is a recurring theme. If the teacher cannot improve sufficiently, you will have to move to formal support, sometimes known as capability procedures. Your LA should guide you about this. It is desirable that the teacher being supported has the advice of a professional association representative. If they are not a member of one, urge them in writing to become one – be sure they cannot accuse you of failing to support them, bringing a case of unfair or constructive dismissal against you. Keep detailed notes of all meetings and make sure the teacher signs a copy as a true record of what happened. Keep notes of any parental complaints – if parents complain orally ask them to put it in writing – you may need the evidence later. If you meet the teacher with their union representative, you may be advised to have someone from HR with you (or a senior member of staff). Most union reps want the best for children as well as their members and will be honest in the support they offer, even to the point of suggesting their client is not suited to the profession. All of this will take a toll on you. You need to look for support from your senior staff.

Other staff may think you are being unduly hard and victimising a hapless colleague (and possibly fearful that you have a hit list and they are next). You did not come into headship to be liked but to ensure that children get the best possible deal. It may help to separate the professional from the personal. This means getting over the message 'You are a good person but a poor teacher.' Remember that you may be doing the person a favour. They may be struggling with the role for a variety of reasons – their parents were teachers and they had a yen to do the same, they need the money – and they may be grateful that you are saying 'This job is not for you.'

Others will fight tooth and nail. In some respects that makes it easier for you, especially if you know they are not up to the job. If there is another local head who has experienced the procedures, see if they would be willing to offer you their perspective. Ensure that you are not the only one evaluating the quality of teaching – your observations could be triangulated with those of a senior teacher, or you could buy in an LA inspector. It is a costly process in terms of time, emotion and money but it is vital that you do not shirk it. Heads have to do hard things sometimes.

Well-poisoners and other characters

Beware of the time-servers. There is a section of the profession who believe you have to put in the years, preferably in several different settings, to prove your mettle. Codswallop. Some of the best teachers and leaders I have seen have been ready for senior positions within a year or two of starting. They will continue to improve and will gain from experience, but if you are looking for an assistant head and you have someone who ticks all the boxes, are you going to pass them over because they have been teaching for only two or three years? The question is 'Can they do the job well?' Ten years working in a mediocre setting with poor role models would not fit you for promotion. Conversely two years in an excellent setting with accomplished and skilled role models may ripen you for a senior position. People will say stupid things like 'She's very ambitious.' I like ambition. I like the strivers and the go-getters, providing they can back it up. The time-servers and plodders may get there in the end, but we need quality people for our children now and we should take the very best forward with us.

Sometimes a job only has to be done well enough – perfection is a huge time-waster. Think of the children who write a sentence, rub it out, then write it again, then rub it out ... Nothing is achieved.

Dealing with grief

On a number of occasions I have 'talent spotted' a teacher and developed and trained them in the arts of headship. They have become indispensable to me. They have my complete trust and play a key role in running the school. They lighten my load and bring a smile to my face.

And then they leave. They get promotion by moving to another school and you are delighted for them – it's what you have been training them for – but you miss them terribly. It is a little like grieving, for they'll never return. But you will already have turned your attention to succession planning and will have someone waiting in the wings to do a similar job (it's never identical because different people bring different things to a role). The mark of a great leader is how many leaders they leave behind.

The function of leadership is to produce more leaders, not more followers.

Ralph Nader

Excellent, well-motivated teachers

Be sure to hang on to 'em!

- Tell them frequently how good they are and how important they are to the school's work.
- Develop them through performance management by ensuring they have great training opportunities in your school, in other schools or on LA/NCSL courses.
- Value them through the salary structure if possible.
- Make sure governors know how good they are, so when it comes to retaining them governors are on board.
- Allow them as much flexibility as possible to maintain their work–life balance. Make sure they know they can occasionally take time off for family reasons. I had one teacher who thought she couldn't attend a friend's wedding because it entailed travelling on a Friday in term-time. I insisted she went and covered her class myself. That flexibility and consideration was repaid many times over.

Working with governors

Be honest and open – with parents, staff, governors and children. If your exam results are poor, tell the governors. When the LA inspector tells them, they can say 'We already know, and this is what we're doing about it.'

I was once told by a new staff governor that I looked bored throughout parts of a meeting. That was a failing on my part. If a governor likes to talk at length about the importance of having copious written guidelines on how children should board and disembark from a coach on a day trip to the zoo, it is my duty to listen as though riveted. A new headteacher should not display anything other than respect to all members of the governing body. And as with staff, build alliances to secure your position.

In a primary school a key relationship is that between the headteacher and the chair of governors.

In a primary school a key relationship is that between the headteacher and the chair of governors. You must be absolutely open and frank with the chair as they will be your greatest advocate. They should never find out bad news from anyone other than you, and they should be kept fully informed about all major events and decisions. A good chair will listen, offer advice and talk through the issues with you. You need to hold on to the good governors and, together, groom the next chair so you don't get one who will undermine the good work you are trying to do.

You also need to build alliances with other members. Governors fall into three camps: the good, the bad and the indifferent.

Good ones: They are public spirited and volunteer because they want to put something back into the community. They are knowledgeable in their own field and will challenge and support you and the school. They are a sounding board for your thoughts and will always lend a sympathetic, though hopefully not uncritical, ear. They have the children at the heart of their thinking and will be doughty defenders of the school.

Bad ones: They may be public spirited, but may come with axes to grind. They are irritatingly monomaniacal about their hobby horses (usually something peripheral, like haircuts and litter) or just barmy (convinced that teachers should volunteer to run school clubs until 9 each evening). They expect you to be an uncritical listening post and have themselves at the heart of their thinking. They will blame you at the first sign of trouble.

Indifferent ones: They can't be bothered, and neither can I.

The clerk to the governors can make meetings run smoothly or become a nightmare of procedural nonsense. A good clerk will advise on procedure before or, discreetly, during the meeting, and will assist the chair in keeping the meeting flowing. When a clerk speaks to the meeting more than some of the governors, it's time to find a new one.

If you are not yet a head but aspire to be one, it is helpful to have experience of governing body meetings as an elected representative or a co-opted (invited) governor. If neither of those avenues is open, ask the chair if you may sit in on a few meetings to see how they work. You may be surprised by the formal procedures, but getting to know them will stand you in good stead.

Managing governors is subject to similar principles to managing other groups. You encourage and build alliances with the good ones, nurturing their talents and encouraging their support. The bad ones you improve – which is difficult as you don't see the governors often – or bypass or remove. Governors may be difficult to remove, but familiarise yourself with the rules as it may be your only option. Most bad governors, once outflanked, will resign anyway. As with staff, it is best to concentrate on getting recruitment right in the first place. You don't recruit governors, but you can discreetly encourage helpful and supportive parents to apply for a vacancy. You can suggest nominees as your LA representatives (such as friendly inspectors, parents or grandparents, local business people).

Make sure governors' meetings have timed agendas to ensure they do not overrun like the parish council from the Vicar of Dibley.

Make sure governors' meetings have timed agendas to ensure they do not overrun like the parish council from the *Vicar of Dibley*. Meetings should take place in school time or immediately afterwards, not from 7 to 9 p.m. If you can't avoid 7 to 9 p.m. meetings, ask the governors to agree that you and any staff present may come to school a little later next morning. Don't let the full governing body meeting revisit everything from the subcommittees – the point of subcommittees is to cut the workload and make better use of time.

If you have difficulty approaching your governing body about any of this – if they're particularly punctilious or grumpy, that is – photocopy this page and stick it in their in-tray.

Attendance

Governing bodies can be especially effective in dealing with a thorny issue such as attendance. It is usually true that happy children don't truant, and reasons for a truanting child's unhappiness may lie at home rather than school. Nonetheless, the statistics will be nailed to your head and you will have to answer such questions as 'What have you done to encourage attendance?' and 'What have you done to chase up persistent absences?'

Any child with attendance that falls below 85 per cent may have their attendance monitored by a governors' pastoral committee. A governor may be nominated to support the parent/carer through an informal meeting, at which it is explained that if the situation doesn't improve, there will be a formal referral to the educational welfare service or truancy officer. The latter may choose to prosecute, though I have grave reservations about imprisoning the parent of a truant.

Quite often the informal presence of a supportive governor will yield useful information that enables you to plan with the parent to reduce absences. You may discover that the child is scared of their teacher or is being bullied. You may find that the parent has problems – from disorganisation to substance abuse – that make it difficult for the child to attend school.

The children who are most often persistently late are sometimes the ones who live in the same road as the school. The factor here is human nature – the source of a lot of the problems you encounter as a headteacher.

Incentives for good attendance:

1. Governors could award a weekly or half-termly attendance cup for the class/year with the best attendance, presenting healthy snacks to any child attaining 100 per cent attendance in a term.
2. Good class attendance each week could be rewarded by extra playtime/ ICT/PE or whatever.
3. Post the names of 100 per cent attenders online.

Try to remove the barriers to punctuality. Be explicit about the link between good attendance and high attainment.

When I was at primary school, late-comers had to line up outside the head's door to receive a thwack of the strap on the hand to encourage punctuality. It was usually the parents' fecklessness that the children were being punished for. Make sure that attendance measures target parents. Try to remove the barriers to punctuality. Be explicit about the link between good attendance and high attainment. Make it clear that some children will otherwise not be able to access the rewards of punctuality, and that would be unfair.

Relating to parents

What will you set out to achieve in your first hundred days of headship, and what will be the key actions to bring this about? One of your first tasks is to establish credibility with parents:

- From day 1 get out before and after school and mingle – don't stand in one place. Smile, greet them, and show that you are comfortable to be with them. Join the school-gate gossips. It's amazing what you will find out.
- Get a newsletter out stating that you are interested in hearing what they like about the school and what they would like to change. Explain that this is a consultation, not a guarantee. Often you will be able to act on their advice, sometimes you will be unable to, and occasionally you will not want to.
- Get parents into assembly so they can see the good work their children do.
- Make sure communication systems are appropriate and working effectively – text-messaging systems can cost as little as £700 a year and are a great way to contact hard-to-reach or busy parents.
- Have open afternoons so they can see classrooms in action.
- Make sure the PTA is a good ambassador for the school.
- The parents are part of the hand you've been dealt. Live with them. What are you going to do to make your school great for your children, so that when they cross the threshold each morning they know they will be safe, will be allowed to learn, will be happy and will develop their potential?

> When they leave aged 11 they will be able to access the next stage of their education with motivation and a love of learning.

Without the confidence of the parents you're in trouble. If parents start voting with their feet you lose children, you lose budget and you lose staff. You need to listen (but see below for meeting parents en masse) and set out how you intend to address any concerns. Never promise anything you might not be able to deliver. Always promise to look into a suggestion and get back to the parent within a set time-frame. Make sure you stick to it.

Parents have a view. They are children's first and most important teacher. Their word of mouth is the best advert for your school that you can get.

Parents have a view. They are children's first and most important teacher. Their word of mouth is the best advert for your school that you can get. Ignore them or alienate them at your peril. You will have to educate them in what you are striving to achieve for them and their children; your vision needs to be explicit and clearly communicated to all members of the school community.

Dealing with individual angry parents

Simply listen, and maybe make notes. Clarify through questioning, refraining from questioning the validity of what they are saying. Undertake to investigate any other angles and get back to them before the end of the day or a prearranged time. Stick to this – if the issue isn't resolved by then call them to tell them that.

Angry parents – in a mob

If a group of parents want to see you en masse about some issue, it is almost always best to avoid the situation. In one incident a child was beckoned to come to the playground railings by a stranger. Uproar followed when this came to light. No harm had come to the child, but parents were rightly concerned about preventing future occurrences. The head agreed to meet a group of about 20 parents. She explained what had happened and what steps had been taken, very quickly, to avoid repetition. The parents did not listen, and there was something quite primitive about it. The head never stood a chance. If she'd said there were to be armed guards patrolling the perimeter they would not have been satisfied. The moral is, always meet discontented parents individually to explain and assuage – preferably following a reassuring newsletter message. Avoid meeting them together when mob mentality might take hold. (The same holds true for irate staff. Always pick them off one by one.)

> ASDA supermarkets have a display at the entrance to their shops saying how they have responded to customers' suggestions: 'You told us ... We have ...' – simple, visual, explicit, interactive. You could do the same on your website and/or your Virtual Learning Environment.

Parent surveys

Use the Ofsted one or devise your own more exciting, more human one. What do you want to find out? How good is communication? Do they think their child is well cared for? What are their expectations of us?

A survey might look like this:

	always	sometimes	hardly ever	never
My child enjoys lessons	☐	☐	☐	☐
School keeps me well informed about progress	☐	☐	☐	☐
I feel my child is happy and safe at school	☐	☐	☐	☐
The teachers treat my child fairly	☐	☐	☐	☐

When being inspected by Ofsted, issue the completed parent survey as part of a newsletter to parents highlighting the good things about your school, saying, 'These are some things about our school that you have told us you really like. Why not tell the Ofsted team about them?'

Collate findings; always offer an open-ended response too ('Anything else you would like us to know?'); allow anonymity; report to governors and staff, and publish the findings to parents.

Web survey or focus groups

Select a dozen or so parents at random from a year group, key stage or whole school. Invite them in to discuss the school's progress with governors. This fulfils the governor's remit of consultation. Parents may open up to non-teaching figures, giving the governors a chance to find out direct how parents feel the school is serving them and their children. Anonymity could be guaranteed. Questions – or areas of questioning – should be agreed by the governing body, based on their self-evaluation. Ask only about things you need to find out. Results should be fed back to staff and other governors, and should be included in your self-evalution form (SEF). The exercise could be repeated in 6 or 12 months' time to see if concerns raised have been addressed successfully.

'The children are delightful', a colleague once confided in me. 'It's their parents who are difficult.' However your parents are – awkward or supportive – they are all you have. Learn to work with them and encourage them to work with you.

Top five complaints about parents by headteachers

They do nothing to help their child learn. They tell me 'You get paid to teach 'em to read – I don't.'
They complain at the drop of a hat.
They keep their child off when they – not their child – are ill.
They take their child on holiday during term-time, thereby skewing my absence figures.
They send their child to school inappropriately dressed.

Parents tend to come in when they need to complain and keep away when they're happy – they occasionally come in to say 'Well done', but not quite so readily – if they're happy they feel no need. If teachers get on to the playground at the start and finish of each day to share good news with parents about their child, rather than telling them when their child has done something wrong, this can help to change the culture to a much more positive two-way exchange.

Let's look at one of those areas. How often do they complain and what are they complaining about? Log the complaints and your responses. Are their

Complaining parents fall into two camps: those with a genuine, unresolved grievance; and those for whom laying the cloths of heaven at their feet would be insufficient.

complaints reasonable – you may be so embroiled that you need to ask a governor for their opinion on this. Are your responses appropriate and effective? If they are not, the parent will keep complaining. Have you asked a parent governor to mediate? Complaining parents fall into two camps: those with a genuine, unresolved grievance; and those for whom laying the cloths of heaven at their feet would be insufficient (apologies to W.B. Yeats). With a genuine unresolved grievance, have you listened, demonstrated your empathy and told them how you intend to act? Above all, be objective – never dismiss a parent's concerns out of hand.

How not to deal with a complaint

Parent: I'm worried that my child's teacher isn't treating her fairly. (trans.: My child's teacher is a vindictive bully.)

Head: I'm sure Miss Blossom would never do that. (trans.: How dare you come in here accusing my staff of vindictiveness?)

Parent: Well, she is very abrupt with me when I speak to her, has never given my child a merit in two terms and called her 'stupid' in front of the other children. (trans.: I'm telling you, matey, she's a vindictive bully!)

Head: I'm sure it can be explained. I'll talk to her about it. (trans.: I don't believe a word of it and I'm saying this to make you go away.)

How to deal with a complaint better

Parent: I'm worried that my child's teacher isn't treating her fairly. (trans.: My child's teacher is a vindictive bully.)

Head: That must be worrying for you. Can you be more specific? (trans.: I'm listening and recognise it must be serious for you to come and see me. I'm taking you seriously and would be interested to hear more.)

Parent: Well, it might be me, but she is very abrupt when I speak to her, has never given my child a merit in two terms and called her 'stupid' in front of the other children. (trans.: You're being nice but your teacher is definitely a vindictive bully!)

Head: They're pretty serious things and certainly need looking into. I will talk to the teacher and your child and, if necessary, other children in the class and get back to you by the end of the day to let you know what I've found out. What's the best number to ring you on at 4 p.m.? (trans.: I'm listening, I'm taking you seriously, I'm going to investigate. I'm going to call you to let you know what I've found out and what I intend to do about it.)

While 99 per cent of parent complaints need to be taken seriously, very occasionally you will have a parent who wants the attention that complaining gets them.

How not to deal with axe grinders

Parent: I'm worried that my child's teacher isn't treating her fairly. (trans.: My child's teacher is a vindictive bully.)

Head: I thought we'd resolved that issue last month (trans.: Oh no, not you again!)
Parent: Well it's been happening again. My Laura was given a blunt pencil to write with and then got told off for having bad handwriting! (trans.: I get a kick out of the attention you give me and will complain that the teacher made the weather bad if given half a chance.)
Head: I'll check with your child's teacher. (trans.: Please go away.)

How to deal with axe grinders better

Parent: I'm worried that my child's teacher isn't treating her fairly. (trans.: My child's teacher is a vindictive bully.)
Head: I thought we'd resolved that issue last month (trans.: Oh no, not you again!)
Parent: Well it's been happening again; my Laura was given a blunt pencil to write with and then got told off for having bad handwriting! (trans.: I get a kick out of the attention you give me, and will complain that the teacher made the weather bad if given the chance.)
Head: I have a note here of the complaints you've made. Because I take them seriously I keep a record of them – I want Laura to be happy. Each time I've found that there was nothing to answer or you'd exaggerated things. My teaching staff are disappointed that they're spending time on such issues when they could be using it to help your child. (trans.: Gotcha!)
Parent: They never help my Laura. They don't like her. (trans.: Rumbled.)
Head: You've had a chance to speak to the chair of governors, I know. She and I are concerned that we are not living up to the standards you require for your daughter and were wondering, in your child's best interests, whether her needs might be better met at another local school. (trans.: Sling your hook; your child is happy and making progress – she'd make more progress if you found a different hobby from complaining.)

Parents have a right to good communication from the school. They have a responsibility to communicate well in return.

If parents are verbally or physically aggressive or threatening, you can ban them from the premises, which includes the playground. If necessary involve the police: a parent whom you have banned is trespassing if they turn up. Notes on any incidents should be retained. It helps to display posters explaining that threatening or violent behaviour will not be tolerated.

Parents' top five complaints about schools

Poor communication – in particular about their child's progress.
The teacher is victimising or treating their child unfairly.
Poor behaviour.
Poor results.
Homework – too much or too little.

Parents have a right to good communication from the school. They have a responsibility to communicate well in return – contact details, absences and the like. Issues like this could be covered in your home–school agreement, a statutory policy that many schools have neglected.

Poor behaviour, quite apart from being morally deplorable and debilitating for all concerned, is public relations poison for a school. If you don't get it right, you might as well shut up shop.

Homework is something that will never please everyone, so don't get distracted by it. There is little evidence that homework has a significant positive effect on a child's academic performance up to age 11. The best homework is simply to read as many great books as they can and learn multiplication and division facts by heart. Children need a home life, not more school in the evenings. Homework is only ever as good as the parent who has helped them do it.

Make sure your complaints policy is up to date – if necessary borrow someone else's and tweak it to suit your school. Be aware that a parent, after complaining to the LA, can take an issue to the secretary of state.

Developing the children

Establish credibility with children

At well as winning the confidence of parents, you have to gain the confidence of the children. You start with an inbuilt advantage. You are the headteacher and that automatically comes with a certain amount of status and image. But beware, that will vanish if you make a hash of things. You start with capital in the form of goodwill and expectation, and you need to invest it wisely.

You start with capital in the form of goodwill and expectation, and you need to invest it wisely.

When you visit classes, get down and talk to them. Find out their names – learn ten a day and in just over month or so you'll know the name of every child in a school of 300. School management systems often include photos, so you can swot in your office. When in the playground, find out what the dynamics are. Make your assemblies something they look forward to. Some heads do conjuring tricks, play a musical instrument or are stand-up comics. Not all of us have such skills, but telling a good story is a not an unreasonable expectation. Keep it brief – remember how numb your bottom can get when you sit on a hall floor. Stand by the school gate at the end of the day and bid them goodbye – with a smile on your face – as they leave.

The school council

The school council has become a must-have school accessory, along with water coolers and outdoor classrooms (education is as subject to fashion as anything else). If you don't use it, you might as well not have one. Be wary of overreliance on the school council as a means of utilising pupil voice – I find it preferable to spread the net wider for that.

The school council gets the children's involvement and ideas on things that really matter – such as learning and well-being. Things like whether football should be allowed before school and taking part in a charity event are perhaps more peripheral.

Seven things to seek the school council's opinion on:

1 What one thing do teachers do that helps you feel happy?
2 What two things do teachers do to help you learn?
3 What is the main thing that stops you learning?
4 How might we remove that barrier?
5 Are school meals good value?
6 What use could we make of our grounds?
7 If you could change just one thing in the school, what would it be?

Questions relating to the five outcomes of Every Child Matters (ECM) are fruitful starting points for discussion.

School council members should be invited to governors' meetings to offer their views – perhaps the first meeting each term. Use them or lose them – if you never address what they've told you, they will soon stop telling you.

Pupil lesson observation

Children can be astute observers of what goes on in a classroom. When we have a new supply teacher in, I ask a couple of children after an hour or so 'What's the teacher like?' Comments will range from 'They can't control us' to 'They are really kind.' In my current school we have asked pairs of children to sit in on lesson observations, usually with a prompt sheet, and then have a discussion with the adult observers afterwards. Their views are perceptive and pertinent.

Prompts for pupil lesson observations

What did the children learn in that lesson that they didn't already know?
What did the teacher do to help that happen?
What do you think needs to be done to help the children do better?
How fair was the teacher with the children?
What were the children doing most of the time?
What was the best part of the lesson?
Which bits of the lesson did not work quite so well?
What could have made that better?

Pupils also sit in on the selection of new staff members, preparing some questions for candidates in advance.

Reviewing

At the end of your first week it is salutary to make a list. If you're one of those people who are really hard on themselves, you probably feel you've achieved nothing. A list will show you have. If you are an irrepressible optimist you may feel you've done brilliantly. A list will show you what you have done; you can make a list of what you still have to do.

Take stock, reflect and plan. Then consign the first list to a mental box labelled 'Not to be opened till Monday'. Leave work no later than 5 p.m. Over the weekend replenish your energy by giving yourself whatever treat might seem appropriate and legal. Improving schools is tough work and you are the person leading it, so you need to be well rested before your second week starts.

Chapter 4 Distributed leadership and building capacity

Farewell to superhead – hello, distributed leadership

We have got rid of chalk and of corporal punishment, but we are still hidebound by traditional hierarchies in school.

We have got rid of chalk and of corporal punishment, but we are still hidebound by traditional hierarchies in school. It is not always appropriate and certainly it is not appropriate all of the time. It generally looks something like this:

HEADTEACHER
DEPUTY HEADTEACHER
SENIOR TEACHERS (TLR / ASSISTANT HEADS)
CLASS TEACHERS

It's a vertical system with the head firmly in control and the class teachers at the bottom. It works most of the time and is useful on occasion. But there are other ways. How does this look?

HEADTEACHER DEPUTY HEADTEACHER SENIOR TEACHERS
PROJECT MANAGING CLASS TEACHERS / CLASSROOM ASSISTANTS
CLASS TEACHERS AND OTHER ASSISTANTS

It's still hierarchical, but it's flatter. A flatter system allows leadership to be distributed amongst a team and even, to some extent, to those outside the leadership team. Authority in line with the school's agreed vision can be exercised by the whole team or a subgroup (usually the SLT).

Or how about this one?

PROJECT-LEADING TEACHING ASSISTANT
HEADTEACHER DEPUTY HEADTEACHER SENIOR TEACHERS ETC.

In this model a clearly defined project is being led by a non-teaching assistant – there is no need for the head to be involved apart from in setting the parameters. The model is based on delegation rather than distribution.

The job of headteacher is too big for one person or even for the leadership team, and can be fulfilled only if others share the load. If you believe that everyone in a school has leadership potential – including the children – you can develop a strategy to build leadership depth. School improvement becomes more manageable and also more long lasting and easier to sustain, even when staff changes take place, as they inevitably do. A school that successfully distributes leadership at all levels is one that is reflective and risk-taking, and that has a highly motivated and valued staff.

The test of how effectively leadership is distributed is in the question 'What happens if the head falls under a bus?' In a traditional school all responsibility for leadership would immediately fall to the deputy. If there were a serial killer pushing teachers under buses and the deputy went next, the school would be vulnerable. In a school where leadership is distributed, everything would carry on much as normal because it would not be reliant on individuals, but on collegiality and teamwork. The superhead, parachuted into failing schools to rescue them, was only ever a media invention, good for a headline or two. What we are with now is highly effective and self-sustaining teams.

Leadership responsibility can be distributed to those with ability and capacity to lead, whether they are a clerical assistant (CA) or a teacher with a year's experience.

Be wary of borrowing a distributed leadership model from a successful school. You always need to tweak or redesign to ensure it will work in your context. There are times when you will have to adopt a more autocratic model ('Thou shalt ...' moments, I call them) if non-negotiables need to be brought into play. In fact, as a head you will need a repertoire of different leadership styles.

In a traditional hierarchy there is a head, a deputy or an assistant or two, some middle leaders, then the class teachers. Below come the support staff. The head holds the power and influence and dispenses it with a greater or lesser degree of magnanimity through the organisation. All decisions are referred back up the chain of command and there is a tendency by those at the top to micro-manage – deciding on everything from toilet paper to staff promotions. Advantages are few, disadvantages are legion. Decision-making is slow and cumbersome, an atmosphere of fear based on favouritism and deference often prevails, and when the head falls under that bus while thinking which toilet rolls to buy, the organisation is left with no one empowered to take over.

The best leaders are judged by how many new leaders they create and leave behind them to serve their own organisation and others in the community. These heads are non-hierarchical and work from flatter management structures. Roles are delegated clearly and lines of accountability are set out. Leaders are grown systematically and trained so that leadership is genuinely and effectively distributed. Clarity of vision and unanimity of purpose, together with the centrality of the SIP, means that there is a synergy about decision-making. All leaders are able to make judgements and take decisions that they know are in line with the head's thinking – they keep the head fully informed but don't have to seek permission to dot every i and cross every t.

The head is not the most important person in the school – the children are that – but in the relationships the head enables and the vision they lead they set the tone for all the school does. They are first among equals: the buck stops there but others get to bash it about a bit.

I used to do all the work-sampling. It sounds grand but it's just having a look to see if the children are about where they should be. Now all the work-sampling is done by subject managers and they report back to teachers and to me. I am still finding out – I do initial samples with new subject managers to moderate judgements and ensure accuracy – but I am not doing all the work. I have empowered others to do it, something that can go on their CV and stand them in good stead when they go for their next promotion.

I used to do lesson observations on my own. Now I always do it as one of a pair. We moderate each other's judgements and I am training others. I have a like-minded team of experts who are developing themselves and relieving me of day-to-day monitoring and evaluation in order to concentrate on the bigger strategic picture.

How do you decide who does what – and what they should do with it when they've done it?

Don't waste time on things you don't need to do. If you are spending the day indoors there is no need to watch or listen to a weather forecast. If your focus is reading there is no point in spending time in looking at drawing in DT. It is not necessary, so why bother?

What you do and who does it and – most importantly – why, should be set out clearly in your SIP, together with timings and arrangements for monitoring effectiveness and impact. It is good policy to report findings to governors in writing or orally. Governors can play a pivotal role in ensuring the school remains focused on the core aspects of its improvement plan.

What is distributed leadership?

I first heard of distributed leadership as 'bobbing corks' – leaders rising to the surface to take particular responsibilities. It is to some extent the opposite of the superhead model (the downside of which is that it does not purposely develop leadership in others, so schools often revert to failure once a superhead has flown off to rescue another school in need). I wrote earlier – and Machiavelli wrote even earlier – that heroic leadership is not sustainable because the job is not do-able by one person. Distributed leadership embodies concertive action – Take That as a group was more successful than any of the individuals in it. The whole is greater than the sum of the parts.

Distributed leadership embodies concertive action – Take That as a group was more successful than any of the individuals in it.

Why distribute leadership?

1 Succession planning. Ralph Nader said leaders should be judged by how many other leaders they develop.
2 Empowering others, releasing their capacity and developing skills they need to become leaders in their own right.

3 Helping to achieve better work–life balance, sharing the load so that real and lasting improvement can be achieved.
4 Increasing the likelihood of alignment on vision amongst the stakeholders.
5 More likelihood of sustaining performance at a high level.

Some heads like to keep all the leadership power, not even delegating to the caretaker the power to order brooms. They have to have their fingers prised off the wheel of power with a crowbar. These leaders will never develop other leaders – a waste for head, school and other potential leaders.

Others may have only just got power and want to play with it for a bit before giving it away. That is understandable. It takes bravery and willingness to take a risk to invest power that is yours in others. Sensible leaders hire staff who could be as clever or cleverer than themselves. They know that the long-term needs of the school and the children are more important than their own glorification. For the school to achieve real success it needs a great team. Great headteachers are ambitious for the school – not for themselves – and have the will to make it happen, whatever it takes.

The head to whom I was deputy spawned seven or eight future headteachers from her staff – a great legacy in terms of influencing children's education and their life chances. I want to do the same.

Delegation and distribution

You instruct your assistant to work-sample a teacher's literacy work on a given date because of concerns about expectations and standards. You request a written report and verbal feedback. You decide on a plan of action to improve the situation. A month later you repeat the exercise to check for improvements. You report on progress to the governing body. You are firmly in control. But without you the system falls apart.

Your assistant comes to you to say that she has done a sample of a teacher's literacy work as part of her regular routine check on standards and expectations. She tells you why she was concerned about what she found and says she has fed back clearly to the teacher, will check on progress regularly over the next month, and keep you informed. You are still in control but you have developed real independence and leadership in your assistant. Without you the system will carry on.

Delegation is not a high-order leadership skill, distribution is. The aim is for staff to become self-directed rather than other directed.

Business leader Sir Gerry Robinson appointed good staff and trusted them to get on with it. When running Granada, he generally left the office by 5 and sometimes took Fridays off – he says 'People who cannot leave work at a reasonable time are either kidding themselves or disorganised.'

You can only march with the army you've got, so you need to find out the skills and attributes of your current team – including assistants, clerical staff and governors.

1 Identify

Do a staff self-audit. Find out which of your bobbing corks have potential and are ready to float to the surface.

When appointing NQTs look for future leaders within your own school and others, to secure succession planning. Ask yourself 'Does this person have the qualities necessary to run a school seven or eight years hence?'

2 Train

Leadership training needs to be made explicit. Leadership is developed through in-house and external training. Techniques and methods are clearly taught: how to evaluate someone else's lesson, how to work-sample, networking, how to present, interpersonal skills, and so on.

Core subject leaders are paired on an apprenticeship model – workload, knowledge and training are shared and you have in-built succession planning.

Vision must be made explicit and the SIP has to be central to everything done in the school. Then there is synergy in leadership and less likelihood of rogue decisions. Everyone knows what is expected of them and why. Communication needs to be top quality and two-way.

Give them all the opportunities to lead that they want – much of this will be about training, not payment. One of the best teachers I ever worked with, now a leader in another school, used to ask for additional opportunities. I have a classroom assistant who has an interest in and eye for design, so she evaluates and organises everything from curtains to lighting in the school.

3 Encourage and nurture

We need to be a good advert for aspiring headteachers and set out why it's a great job.

Sell leadership as a great thing to do. Headship gets a bad press – it's said to be stressful and the accountability is daunting. We need to be a good advert for aspiring headteachers and set out why it's a great job. If we constantly look downcast about our work, why should anyone else consider taking it on?

Staff are encouraged to take calculated risks and are given a great deal of autonomy. Forgive them when they fail – once or twice. Help them to learn from their mistakes. Tell them how wonderful they are and that they'll be running their own school one day. They will feel encouraged to deliver and know that their contribution is valued because you tell them – frequently.

Work–life balance should be given high status. Respect their entitlement to a family life and model that behaviour yourself, even if your family is just you and the goldfish. This is behaviour that you must model yourself.

In my version of distributed leadership there are parameters. In terms of accountability, the buck still stops with me. Where there are no parameters, decision-making can be delayed. There will be times where autocratic leadership and hierarchical models are appropriate, depending on where the school's development is at.

For those that say 'Whom am I going to distribute it to?', the advice is to look for the leadership in your existing staff and ensure new appointees are capable of it. It is your job, your pleasure and your privilege to unearth, nurture and develop leadership. Begin training your staff in leadership skills and set rigid hierarchies to one side.

Chapter 5 School improvement planning for dummies

Fluid mechanics in relation to flight dynamics, and aeroelasticity in the field of avionics, are seen by some as essential to ...

20% is knowing what to do – 80% is making sure it gets done

I'm sorry. For some reason I was talking rocket science. Thankfully, school improvement planning isn't rocket science. It simply requires analysis, clarity and lots of graft.

School improvement planning is about maintaining and developing the good things and improving the substandard things to make the school better for the children. It's about a combination of change and continuity: beware of throwing out the baby with the bathwater. At its most straightforward it is a relatively simple cycle:

- Find out where you are now: effectiveness of teaching and learning, ECM, standards and so on.
- Find out how you compare with similar schools that are using benchmarking information.
- Plan what you need to do to perform as well as the best of these similar schools – no excuses.
- Implement the plan.
- Review it and return to Go.

Where are we now?

Monitoring is of little value without evaluation.

We know where we are now because we monitor and evaluate. Monitoring is of little value without evaluation. It would be like the doctor telling you 'Yes, you have a sore throat' without telling you what's causing it and what to do about it.

- We use RAISEonline data to analyse and question our performance and the performance of subgroups. We know how children have performed in end-of-key-stage assessments and how subgroups (free school meals, SEN needs, black and minority ethnicity) have performed. RAISEonline data show us how we compare with similar schools. Contextual value-added data (CVA) are flawed and no comparison will be absolutely fair, but they enable you to raise questions about your school's performance. If you are achieving as well as similar schools in maths and science but underperforming in English, you might want to ask why. Is it your curriculum, the time you give to it, leadership of that area, a particular teacher or group?

- We use our own internal tracking data to review the progress of individuals, groups and teachers in English, mathematics and science (ICT may replace science as a core subject by 2010). We discuss this and moderate levels of work at regular intervals in staff meeting and PPA time to give teachers a thorough understanding of how children are doing. We know what their target levels are – these are challenging but achievable – and we know how each class and year group is progressing. If individuals, groups or classes are falling short, we find out why and take action.
- We observe lessons and know the quality of teaching and learning that goes on measured against criteria in the school's teaching and learning policies. Written observations are fed back to the teacher and followed up. Good practice is shared and areas for development are highlighted and managed through the performance management process.
- We talk to children about their learning, finding out the main barriers and motivators. We talk to them in pupil-voice interviews about the five outcomes of ECM and use these soft data to evaluate our success.
- We look at samples of their work on regular and planned occasions and, if need be, ad hoc. We feed back on those samples, following up our findings in subsequent sampling.
- We talk to parents to find out their views and use them to plan improvements.

Note the follow-up. For some time I was doing the monitoring and evaluating and not the taking action. I wondered why nothing was improving. Follow-ups are the tough bit – that may be when you say 'Well done, that was much improved' or 'I am concerned that you haven't improved at all.'

The moral purpose of leading a school should never be lost sight of – not moral in the judgemental sense, but moral as in 'Are you doing everything possible to give these children the best start in life?'

As well as the bread and butter of standards you will also glean information about happiness, behaviour, attitudes and much else. All of this will feed into the actions you take. You might, for example, find out that though children are reasonably adept at reading (decoding) and understanding what they read (comprehending), they don't enjoy it much. You will think it's appalling that children are leaving your school without loving to read, so you will plan to inculcate a love of reading in them, knowing that it will have a big impact on how well they learn in all areas.

Planning to improve

You know where you are. You even know how you compare with similar schools. What do you do to make it better? You have identified your main area for improvement – let's say it's about improving enjoyment of reading. Where do you start?

Gather views. Ask people. Explain to parents 'We are trying to improve enjoyment of reading – what do you think might help? How can we help you help your child?' Always make your communications parent friendly and avoid educational jargon – the more you can 'sell' an idea to parents and the better you can explain what's in it for them, the more support you will garner.

What not to say

Reading initiative

Dear parent

We are hoping to improve our SATs score for reading by encouraging our children to read for enjoyment from a wide range of genres. We will be holding a workshop in the school this Thursday to tell you what you can do to improve your own child's enjoyment of reading.

Yours sincerely

K.F. Harcombe (MA)

The title is dull! The first line is what's in it for the school, not for the children. No wonder the children aren't enjoying reading if it's all as pompous as this!

What to say

Help your child be a great reader!

Dear parent

We are proud of the work that our children do in reading and we want them to have a real love of reading to stay with them in life and help them achieve. We have come up with some new ideas to enthuse your child about reading. We should like to share them with you over tea and biscuits this Thursday in school. We know that many of you have great ideas too and we hope you'll be able to share them with us. That way we can work together to ensure our children get a brilliant start in life.

Yours sincerely

Kevin Harcombe
Headteacher

From the start it's about their child, of whom we are proud. We want to share ideas and the tea and biscuits bit indicates it's informal and won't be a lecture. We value their ideas and want to work with them. I'd go to a meeting like that, and I really don't like meetings.

Ask the children

Face-to-face interviews with a selection – random or targeted – are the best way forward, though questionnaires have a place with older children. They will be able to make an important input into most areas. What is it that they like/dislike about reading sessions? You may elicit responses such as they dislike reading at a desk and would prefer a cushion on the floor.

Ask the staff

This is easily done at staff meetings and is a session that the literacy/ communication leader might present – learning support assistants who work with slow progress readers may have useful insights.

Seek advice from other headteachers and/or advisers. Decide what you need to do and what actions you need to take.

Suppose you find that boys aren't attracted by the fiction you offer. A global aim like 'Increasing the number of fiction books read by boys' may need to be broken down into several component parts:

1. Audit current range of boy-friendly books.
2. Ask boys which books they would like us to buy, and buy them.
3. Compare books borrowed at the start of the exercise with books borrowed at the end.
4. Ask boys how they have enjoyed the books and if they have been encouraged to read more.

The actions will need to be time limited. Any costs must be noted and the global aim should have clear and measurable success criteria against which to judge the outcomes. (Targets need to be SMART – specific, measurable, achievable, realistic and time limited.)

Rubbish success criterion

Aim: to improve reading for pleasure amongst boys
Success criterion: boys enjoy reading more

(How will you know? What will it look like?)

Great success criterion

Aim: to improve reading for pleasure amongst boys
Success criterion: Percentage of boys enjoying reading increases from 30% to 60% by July as measured by face-to-face interviews in October and July with cross-sections of abilities. Library-borrowing records shows average borrowing of fiction rises by at least three books a term.

All staff should have buy-in to the SIP by writing a short position statement for their subject/aspect, identifying improvements that took place in the year just ending, improvements they plan to make in the forthcoming year and resourcing they will need to bring about the improvements. Resourcing includes staff meeting time, INSET days, inspector/adviser time, non-contact time and money for books and other equipment. Linking the SIP to the budget is important – auditors and inspectors will expect plans that are costed. At the end of the year governors may want to conduct a cost–benefit analysis of the expenditure. As well as being responsible for their own plans, staff need to be aware of and contribute to the main school improvement priorities.

The SIP should be a regular agenda item at staff and SLT meetings, and a standing agenda item on governing body and subcommittee agendas.

Questions to ask about your SIP

Were the right priorities identified and on what basis?
Are plans addressing the issues that have been identified?
Are plans manageable and affordable?
Are plans, when implemented, having the intended outcomes? How do you know?

You will be checking outcomes in terms of children's work and assessment information regularly. Time flies and it is easy for children to fall behind unnoticed.

Separate your core values and prime purpose – which will never change – from methods and strategies that will change constantly, as everything does. You need clarity about what to do and also about what not to do. When you have followed all the advice in this chapter, check against the sample (p. 44).

School Improvement Plan

Great Primary School *School Improvement Plan 2008–11*

Subject/Aspect English Review of previous plan

- Writing targets were exceeded at KS2 and outstripped any local school. The decision to teach Year 6 as a single cohort with one teacher contributed to this success.
- Writing throughout the school has been evaluated and detailed feedback given to teachers.
- Work is continuing on greater use of formative assessment (Assessment for Learning) to improve children's writing.
- Fischer Family Trust data have been used regularly to ensure challenging group and individual targets.
- In reading, targets were exceeded in both key stages.
- An audit was conducted to find which children were never or rarely heard read by family. Recruited and trained 'reading heroes' from parents. Children who were never heard now have a reading hero three times a week, and children who were rarely heard have a reading hero once a week. This has had an impact on reading age in both key stages.
- In the light of work done in our foundation stage (children covering 44 sounds), phonics teaching in Year 1 has been modified. This has led to a marked improvement in reading levels, with some Year-1 children now achieving levels 2A or 2B consistently in the spring term.
- Our highly successful book week, firstly with children's laureate Michael Rosen, then with Nick Sharratt, raised the profile of reading and writing as fun activities.
- Each child entering Year R was given a book.
- Each child leaving Year 6 was given a book.
- Staff have been positive in their response to changes to the literacy curriculum.
- Beginning to make greater use of pupil voice to improve learning in reading.

Improvement priorities 2008–09:

1. Further raise the profile of reading throughout the school to encourage and motivate children to read.
2. Further improve teaching and learning in writing through more consistent use of AfL.
3. Continue to embed the 'three stories a year' model for children to learn by heart.
4. Review the teaching of spelling.

Priority 1

Actions	When	Who	Costs
Evaluate the new framework and incorporate in planning	From Sept. 09	SL	
Each child to read/listen to a set list of ten books in the course of the year. Also link in to cross-curricular topics and readathon.	From Sept. 08		
Readathon	Nov. 08	SL	
Review Year-2 phonics in the light of progress made in Year R and 1. Adviser to visit in Nov.	From Oct. 08	SL	
Continue to broaden the range of available reading matter by increasing the library stock with a balance of fiction and non-fiction.	From Apr. 08	SL, L	£3,000
Continue half-termly staff meetings – 'What have you done this term to raise the profile of reading?'	Oct. 08	SL, SM	
Evaluate to what extent reading heroes work as a motivator.		SL	0.5 MAST

Priority 1 success criteria

Interview in Apr. 09 (75%) and July 09 (90%): increase in % of children enjoying reading (including 80% boys) from a baseline of 65%

Likely priority 2010: To ensure that 100% of pupils transferring to secondary school have a reading age of at least 9.

Chapter 6
Work–life balance

With a start, I woke up in a cold sweat in the garden. The sun was shining in a cloudless blue sky. Birds were singing. My partner was beside me offering me a cool beer. 'Thank God for that,' I said. 'I've just had the awful nightmare that I spend all my waking hours in school.'

'No,' she replied, 'This is the dream, dear. You've just fallen asleep during your own assembly.' Apologies to Monty Python for adapting a sketch, but some headteachers are living that bad dream. It doesn't have to be that way.

If you are regularly working a 12-hour day, you are probably doing something wrong. Recent data from the School Teachers' Review Body show primary heads working on average a 52-hour week (some are working more than that, some less). Some headships are more demanding than others, but you need to remain in control of hours or you will suffer burn-out.

- The first step is acceptance. Accept that there will always be more to do than you can accomplish in the time given. You have to prioritise. Tasks that take priority are those that will have a direct and positive impact on children's learning – your core activity. Taking part in a sponsored skip may be fun and good for healthy school status, but it won't impress come Ofsted or SATs time. That flyer gets ditched.
- Distinguish between what is urgent and what is important. A child protection incident will be both. Safety and security of children always comes first. On the other hand, an irate parent may demand urgent attention but their complaint may not be important. An email from the LA may be labelled 'Urgent' but mean urgent to them, not to you. Weigh up demands before prioritising them.
- Develop creative delaying tactics. Ask yourself what will happen if something doesn't get done. The government brings in new guidance on assessment. It isn't statutory. You've looked at it and like some of the ideas, but aren't convinced it will have any great impact. All your headteacher colleagues are doing it. Put it in your pending file, find out what colleagues think of it – see Chapter 10 – and when they've ironed out its creases look at it again.
- Leaving work on time is not the sign of a slacker but an indication of professionalism. Colleagues of a friend of mine who works in Europe talk of 'sweatshop Britain'. Here long hours are equated with diligence and effectiveness, but some ineffectual people work long hours and achieve little. Effective workers focus on task completion within a reasonable time and complete the task on time and well. Heads need to model this by leaving at a reasonable hour.

Leaving work on time is not the sign of a slacker but an indication of professionalism.

- Learn to practise the four Ds for prioritising tasks: do, delegate, ditch and delay.
- Sometimes a job has only to be done well enough – perfection is a time-waster.
- Keep a sense of perspective (although, to quote David Brent from *The Office*, 'If you can keep your head when all around you are losing theirs ... you probably haven't fully grasped the seriousness of the situation').

Procrastination is the thief of time, as are staring out of the window, checking emails every five minutes and tidying drawers. Find out where the time goes. The following example is split into one-hour sections, but you could subdivide it into half or quarter hours. Two key aspects of the analysis are the impact on children and whether the task needed to be done by a highly paid superbrain like you. If the impact on children is low and the task could've been done by your PA (writing a newsletter), caretaker (restocking the paper towels) or a pupil (tidying the musical instruments), you've wasted valuable time as well as avoiding or neglecting something more urgent and important. My CA with the eye for design organised new curtains for the hall from drawing up a specification to commissioning the work. This is a task some headteachers might like to do but it is seldom the best use of their time.

Who knows where the time goes?

Complete a time-analysis log for a day. Find out what percentage of time you spend on tasks that have a positive impact on the children, and what percentage is taken up with tasks others could or should do. Score 15 or below and you've just wasted a day. That gives you a starting point for cutting back on time-wasting.

Time-analysis log

Time	Activity	Impact on children (rated1–5, 1 is low impact)	Could this task have been done equally well by someone else? If so, who?
8.00			
9.00			
10.00			
11.00			
12.00			
13.00			
14.00			
15.00			
16.00			
17.00			

Beware quick fixes and snake-oil salesmen

Being a head is hard work and so is being a teacher. Getting standards high and keeping them there can be stressful (and exciting). When the going gets tough, the tendency is to look for miracle cures – just as when a person is seriously ill and conventional medicine has no answers, they will look into remedies based on cod science. Snake-oil salesmen used to roam the Wild West selling patent miracle cures; they are mirrored in current education by pedlars of wares that promise to interest, excite, inspire and raise attainment. They often come couched in scientific or pseudo-scientific language, but the empirical background is invariably weak. The conclusions are stretched into all-embracing philosophies that are sold to heads and teachers at conferences.

Some of it is based on sound common sense or acknowledged medical research. Brain Gym proponents talk about the need to rehydrate to improve concentration – drinking water is common sense. You will find the claims made by some systems perplexing. Be wary of anything you find it hard to relate directly to your children.

A favourite promise of the snake-oil salesmen is 'If you do what you've always done you get what you always get.' It's true, up to a point, but quite often what people say they have done is not what actually has been done. Top-down initiatives are seldom fully adopted and implemented, and teachers and others can sabotage initiatives deliberately, lackadaisically or through incompetence. Remember, only 20 per cent is knowing what to do, 80 per cent is making sure it gets done.

Within-school variation is a greater cause of educational underachievement than variation between schools.

Within-school variation – differences between the quality of teaching and learning in the same school – is a greater cause of educational underachievement than variation between schools. What people say hasn't worked may not have been tried properly. How often have you introduced an initiative at a staff meeting or INSET day and assumed it was being implemented, only to find out later that one or two teachers have not been implementing it with the enthusiasm hoped for? You not only have to know what initiatives to introduce; you need to sell them and, most important of all, to make sure they are happening. Rigorous monitoring, evaluation and follow-up are the best ways to reduce or eliminate within-school variation.

Chapter 7
Dealing with the local authority and other external agencies

You have your own kingdom. The door is closed, you lead and control everything that goes on within and are doing a great job for your children, but there is always someone checking up or interfering – usually from the LA, occasionally (and usually in the form of Ofsted) from central government.

There are a few simple pieces of advice for dealing with these forces. It may be tempting to take a combative approach, but are you willing to accept the distinctly negative outcome of that? That doesn't mean you have to acquiesce and roll over. I suggest a more Machiavellian stand. Employ cunning to make them go away so you can get on with giving children the educational experiences you know they need.

You may receive several visits from what is currently called the School Improvement Partner (formerly adviser, Primary Phase Inspector, etc.), who writes reports on your school and categorises you as outstanding, good, satisfactory or inadequate. Many are fine people – I am one myself – and want to help you, providing they are satisfied you are doing a decent job for the children. For nine years I have had a superb one who knows my school well and has played an active part in moving it forward. With him I always find openness the best policy; he sees my school warts and all and knows how far we have come and what a good job we are doing.

Not all School Improvement Partners are like that. Some clutch a big file and start from the assumption that whoever they are inspecting is lying. They will be inflexible and dogmatic, punctilious and pedantic, and determined on LA advancement.

Sometimes when you are struggling to improve a school, the LA will 'help' you. They do this because they genuinely want you to do the best by the children, they have a statutory responsibility to do so, and the DCFS and Ofsted are standing over them and asking awkward questions like why aren't they closing down failing schools.

They send in the cavalry in the form of consultants, inspectors and advisers. They undoubtedly mean well and occasionally have some of the expertise you need, but they are seldom 'joined up' in their thinking and may offer conflicting advice. Worse, they may have a mantra of 'I can only advise: you need to choose for yourself' – in other words, 'You need to find your own salvation.'

What you most need is time. School improvement does not happen overnight. My own experience indicates that you need up to two years to stop the rot and stabilise the situation, then another two or three to climb up. Buy yourself time by making alliances with the LA representatives that you think will be most likely to support you. You don't need to be besieged by two or three different advisers who visit each week with comments such as 'Good God, how are you going to tackle that?'

It is always better to seek forgiveness than to ask permission – take a risk (a calculated, rational one).

The best inspectors will recognise the conditions in which you are working and strive to give you the time you need, but remember that the supportive ones will not give you time forever. Give them all enough to make them go away at the right time and leave you to get on with improving your school.

How to get rid of inspectors

1 Be nice to them. Don't antagonise. Take them to lunch. Listen to their advice with an eager expression.
2 If their advice supports what you know needs to be done, follow it. If not, put it to the bottom of your in-tray.
3 Build alliances with them. A good LA inspector will be a huge help in batting for you when senior officers might prefer to run you out of town. An alliance is possible if they have a genuine understanding of what you are trying to achieve. Explain it to them.
4 Where there is a difference over strategy, do enough of what they want to make them think you value and will act on their advice. Then do what you really know needs to be done.
5 Never treat them with disdain or take their support for granted.
6 Ofsted inspectors are a special breed. The many good ones can't be hoodwinked, they never miss a trick and they deserve your respect and openness.
7 The few awful inspectors can be hoodwinked, miss a great deal and deserve nothing. Whether they have your respect or not, they have power to derail your work or allow it to run on. They will seldom offer anything in the way of good advice, but will tell you what they think you are doing well and where you fall short.

Keeping track

To help you keep track of all that is going on, you need your own management timetable. A grid that you can use (or adapt) is supplied over the page. An example of how this might be completed appears on the following four pages.

Management timetable

Month	School improvement major initiatives	School development and maintenance tasks	Leadership and management	Staff development	Budgetary cycle	Main school events

Completed management timetable

Month	School improvement major initiatives	School development and maintenance tasks	Leadership and management	Staff development	Budgetary cycle	Main school events
September	E: Continue to evaluate new framework; relaunch retelling of traditional tales; begin issuing reading reward certificates and publish roll of honour in newsletter; teachers retell their favourite stories to class/assembly MA: Review impact of new framework in terms of raising standards MFL: Begin following QCA units of work throughout KS2 Curric.: Check websites for developments in the Alexander Review and Sir Jim Rose's Primary Review and communicate these to staff for discussion. Plan for introduction of aspects of these reviews that can have a positive impact on Redlands children Monitoring/evaluation Leadership team joint lesson obs. throughout school focusing on teacher expectations and AfL Forecasts monitored against FFT type-D expectations	New round of performance management Governing body training Assessment and recording Check timetables for balance, coverage and consistency FSP commences In year teams discuss targets and set for year Analyse SATs outcomes and report to governors Target children identified – those falling below expected level in each year. Lists to Yr leader, HT and DHT Publish list of children on intervention programmes and their current attainment Update target tracker database	Issue curriculum info to parents Leadership and management training for SLT Review SEF at SM	Staff decide staff meeting agendas based on SIP priorities. INSET for planning. Staff book courses from directory and/ or arrange in-house training	Issue salaries notification	
October	E: Review paired reading sessions MA: Arrange parental maths workshops ASS: Implement APP techniques PV: Classroom climate assembly Monitoring /evaluation Work-sampling to evaluate consistency of marking and expectations, focus on consistency of expectation across year groups SENCO evaluate IEPs Planning scrutiny by LT and core-subject leaders Check profiles of attendance data Check profiles of children new to Redlands	Leaflet campaign in playgroups Assessment and recording SATs forecasts analysed and shared with staff Handover dialogue	Tracking update to check pupil progress at staff meeting Evaluate Raiseonline data and Fischer Family Trust (FFT) data	Half-termly staff meetings – 'What have you done this term to raise the profile of reading?'		Maths workshop for parents Parent interviews Open afternoon for prospective parents

Completed management timetable

Month	School improvement major initiatives	School development and maintenance tasks	Leadership and management	Staff development	Budgetary cycle	Main school events
November	E: Ask children and staff for suggestions and purchase new reading-shelf books EY: Review impact of continuous provision PV: Teacher and children to present findings to staff Ask staff to identify one thing they will change about their practice in response to children's findings M: Analyse data from tests so staff build on strengths and address weaknesses. Feed back to individual teachers. Children making less than expected progress identified. These names held by Yr and KS leaders, SLs and HT prog. checked half-termly. Planning shows opportunities for children to chant age-relevant tables in class. Maths homework shows emphasis on learning tables by rote. Parents informed of value of this work and parents and children are aware of X table certificates issued for achievement from R to 6 G&T: Letters to parents regarding the updated able child list/ register. Offer interviews for parents to discuss the needs of their children and update any issues Monitoring/evaluation Evaluate teachers' use of sanctions through scrutiny of HT certificates, spot check of use of smiley faces and scrutiny of hall books SENCO observes lessons in class	Assessment and recording Review targets in year teams RAISE and FFT analysis and report to governors	Early Years meetings SEN meetings Update SEF Leadership and management training for SLT	SM on staff well-being Termly staff meetings – 'What have you done this term to raise the profile of reading?'	Review current budget with a view to eliminating any projected deficit for 09–10	Osmington Bay residential (Year 6) Poppies Shoebox appeal
December	E: Whole-school moderation of the same writing genre; check on progress of retelling classic tales MA: Review impact and progress of AfL in maths through work-sampling Monitoring/evaluation HT sample RED books G&T: Evaluate progress of high attainers in 2, 4, 6 Planning scrutiny by SLs Evaluate progress of children on intervention programmes		Review SATs preparation including forecasts Tracking update to check pupil progress at staff meeting	INSET Staff meeting – 'What have you done this term to raise the profile of reading?'		Christmas bring and buy Concerts and parties Parent-helper mince pies Carol fund-raising

Completed management timetable

Month	School improvement major initiatives	School development and maintenance tasks	Leadership and management	Staff development	Budgetary cycle	Main school events
January 2009	E: Interview children to find current level of interest in reading Curric.: Check websites for developments in the Alexander Review and Sir Jim Rose's Primary Review and communicate these to staff for discussion. Plan for introduction of aspects of these reviews that can have a positive impact on Redlands children Monitoring/evaluation Work-sampling English, mathematics, science – marking, consistency, expectation HT and DHT evaluate preparation for SATs Forecasts monitored against FFT type-D expectations	H&S risk assessment Review and update SIP Assessment and recording Update target tracker database. Forecasts monitored against expectations	Leadership and management training for SLT	INSET	Form-7 census	Curriculum info to parents
February	ASS: Review APP techniques EY: Review impact of continuous provision MFL: Review units of work in KS2 PV: Classroom climate assembly Monitoring/evaluation Lesson obs. throughout school – unannounced Pupil-voice interviews Planning scrutiny IEPs sampled Check profiles of attendance data Check profiles of children new to Redlands	Performance management in year discussions	Open afternoon – Share a Tray Tracking update to check pupil progress at staff meeting		Prepare Price's bid	Share a Tray open afternoon
March	E: Book week? Whole-school moderation of writing genre MA: Review impact and progress of AfL in maths through work-sampling Sust.: Visit other schools in Hants to see sustainability programmes and consider their use here Monitoring/evaluation Cost benefit analysis – ICT HT and DHT review teacher reports Work sample English, mathematics and science Staff evaluate subjects/aspects progress and submit detailed position statements to LMT and governors	Assessment and recording Update target tracker database. Forecasts monitored against expectations	Leadership and management training for SLT Reports home Review SEF at SM	Staff meetings – 'What have you done this term to raise the profile of reading?'	Predict final budget / prepare forward budget Request subject bids	Sponsored bunny bounce Easter celebrations Book week

Completed management timetable

Month	School improvement major initiatives	School development and maintenance tasks	Leadership and management	Staff development	Budgetary cycle	Main school events
April	E: Continue to broaden the range of reading matter available: continue regular reading assemblies to advertise new acquisitions and publicise authors and books PV: Send newsletter to parents to inform them about pupil-voice work Invite parents into school for a presentation led by the CC group outlining the work they have been doing. Reissue questionnaire to quantify improvements and report to governors Curric.: Check websites for developments in the Alexander Review and Sir Jim Rose's Primary Review and communicate these to staff for discussion. Plan for introduction of aspects of these reviews that can have a positive impact on Redlands children Monitoring/evaluation Forecasts monitored against FFT type D expectations	Review and update SIP Issue new prospectus Assessment and recording Final pre-SATs checks	Subject bids and position statements New entrants parents meeting Tracking update to check pupil progress at staff meeting	INSET	Present new budget to governors	Curriculum info to parents
May	MA: Review impact and progress of AfL in maths through work-sampling ASS: Review APP techniques Monitoring/evaluation Evaluate teachers' use of sanctions through scrutiny of HT certificates, spot check of use of smiley faces and scrutiny of hall books G&T: Evaluate progress of high attainers in 2, 4, 6 Planning scrutiny by SLs		SATs and QCA tests		Conduct cost-benefit analysis of selected expenditure	Stubbington residential (Year 4)
June	E: Interview children to find current level of interest in reading; whole-school moderation of writing genre MFL: Review units of work in KS2 PV: Classroom climate assembly Monitoring/evaluation Parental satisfaction questionnaire Analyse and evaluate SATs and other assessments on a class by class, set by set basis	Review individual performance management targets	HT/DHT interview all staff to review year Arrange classes for September QCA results analysis conducted by receiving teachers Leadership and management training for SLT	SINSETM on staff well-being Staff meetings – 'What have you done this term to raise the profile of reading?'		Arts Week Photos Fairthorne Manor residential (Y2) Parent teacher interviews
July	E: Review impact of reading heroes scheme Monitoring/evaluation HT sample RED books	Review SATs against targets	SATs analysis Liaison with secondaries Transfer day and handover records/dialogue Parent interviews Tracking update to check pupil progress at staff meeting.	Half-termly staff meetings – 'What have you done this term to raise the profile of reading?'	Review staff responsibilities and salaries Prepare September prices' bid	Summer fair School sports Leavers' assembly Thanks to parent-helpers Summer reading event Report SATs results to parents

Chapter 8
School self-evaluation

The SEF is a hugely important document. Aside from data, it is the first glimpse Ofsted will have of your school. They will use it to judge how well you know your school and how adept you are at school improvement planning. The requirements of the SEF change regularly, but there are some rules for how you respond to them.

Always focus on impact. You may have held numerous workshops for parents, run booster classes for the children, invested squillions in new technology and produced a Christmas show that would have Andrew Lloyd Webber applauding. If that has had no discernible impact on outcomes, it has been a total waste of time, money and effort.

Your school improvement plan (SIP) should feed into the SEF neatly – some schools use the headings from the SEF as the basis for the SIP. All schools now have a SEF. This following advice will help you revise yours if necessary.

Firstly, it should arise naturally from the day-to-day work of the school. All the monitoring and evaluation you do should feed into it. Your hard (numerical/ quantifiable) and soft (opinion/survey) data should underpin every statement. Evidence is essential – Ofsted will not take your word for it. Don't include the evidence in the SEF; signpost it. Three or four suitably indexed files should do. Remember to update the content of the files when you undertake new monitoring and evaluation, and to update the SEF itself. This could be a clerical job you could entrust to an HLTA/CA, or it could be a joint exercise undertaken half termly at SLT meetings.

Like your monitoring and evaluation timetables, the SEF should be reviewed as part of the cycle of the school year and your evidence files updated accordingly.

To manage the SEF, plan how and when. Mine doubles as my headteacher's report to governors, which saves me writing a separate document each term. For governors I don't reprint the SEF each time as large parts of it do not change. I précis the updates since I last reported. This means governors are familiar with the contents of the SEF when Ofsted comes calling. Like your monitoring and evaluation timetables, the SEF should be reviewed as part of the cycle of the school year and your evidence files updated accordingly. When the Ofsted team drag you out of bed at 3 in the morning, you will be prepared for the event.

Ofsted guidance suggests that the SEF should:

- convey a clear picture of how well the school is doing
- provide proof of how you know what you know
- show what you are doing to build on successes and remedy weaknesses.

Before you submit, read it through and answer the following questions:

1 Is it short and to the point?
2 Have you answered all the questions?
3 Are your judgements clear?
4 Have you reflected stakeholders' views?
5 Does it give a fair and honest picture of what the school is like?
6 Have you been clear about actions being taken to improve?
7 If you were an inspector, what questions would your SEF lead you to ask?

The key is to look at impact. If you have spent time/money/effort doing something and it has had no discernible impact, you have wasted time. Bury it. This is no time to be honourable about your mistakes.

For example if you answer the question 'How much do learners enjoy their education?' positively, writing a long description of happy smiling children bringing teacher an apple each day, the Ofsted inspector may ask why your attendance is below the national average. You will need to acknowledge this fact in your SEF and set out what you are doing, and intend to do, to rectify the situation, as well as what impact that has had. Reward systems? No impact. Parent interviews? Limited impact. Use of attendance officer? Good impact. Demonstrate the range of things you have done and also that you have evaluated the outcomes and adjusted your tactics accordingly. Inspectors know that attendance is a tough nut to crack. They will be looking for evidence that you are taking a robust and sensible approach.

It is better to understate your judgements than to inflate them. If you suspect something may be of outstanding quality, set out the evidence to support this, but be wary of giving yourself the grade. That may smack of arrogance to the inspector.

Test the judgements with:

- your SLT – tell them to challenge any statement they feel is not supported by the evidence or for which the evidence is decidedly thin, or lacking
- staff – do a section a week; they may come up with evidence that you neglected to include or a different slant on the analysis you have undertaken
- governors – perhaps as a standing item on a sub-committee.

Talk through particular sections with a focus group of parents. (The section on views of parents/carers in particular.) In having them check your judgements you are gathering the views of stakeholders – it's a perfect circle!

Children should be consulted about some sections too – or they could come up with their own mini-SEF based on some/all of the ECM outcomes. How do they think we're preparing them for future economic well-being? What things do we do that they feel help them enjoy and achieve?

You could focus on one aspect, such as transition to the next phase of education or from nursery to your EYFS class. Do a parent survey with selected questions, then turn their answers into hard data (see p. 58 and p. 59). That's good practice anyway. You want transition to be as smooth as possible for all your children.

Finally, don't forget the technical section of the form – budget, staffing, number of learners per computer and such. This needs updating slightly less frequently.

Help us make our school even better!

We want to improve our service to parents and children each year, and we should welcome your views on how well we managed your child's induction into the Reception class earlier this year. You can help us make our school even better by letting us know how the process worked for you and your child and by giving us any suggestions you have for improvement. Please talk to your child about how they found it, too.

How beneficial was the initial parents' meeting?

You may like to comment on the format and length of the meeting and whether the information covered everything you needed to know.

How helpful and approachable did you find the Early Years staff throughout the induction process?

Did you have too much / too little contact; were problems resolved quickly enough; were there any teething troubles?

How easy was it for your child to adapt to the routines such as drop-off and pick-up, toileting, break and lunch?

Have you found home–school communication good, bad or indifferent? What might we do to make it better for you?

Have you any further comments?

You may wish to sign this form but you do not have to.

Signed ____________________

Thank you for taking the time to complete this form and helping us to help our children.

Induction survey results

Sample size ______________ Number returned ______________

	Very useful / good	Good	No comment	Not useful / no good
How beneficial was the initial parents' meeting?				
How helpful and approachable did you find the Early Years staff throughout the induction process?				
How easy was it for your child to adapt to routines such as drop-off and pick-up, toileting, break and lunch?				
Have you found home–school communication good, bad or indifferent? What might we do to make it better for you?				

Other comments

Chapter 9
Machiavellian headship

Why sixteenth-century leadership is the way forward

Nicolo Machiavelli was a sixteenth-century Italian writer whose most famous work, *The Prince*, was seen, wrongly, as an amoral guide to leadership. 'Machiavellian' has come to mean something deceitful and ruthless. Your headship should not be deceitful or ruthless (except in pursuit of a better deal for the children), but you should be able to play the game to the advantage of your school. Here is what Machiavelli wrote:

Since the modern state is too complex to be managed by any single human being, the effective ruler will naturally need to have advisers who assist in governance. Choosing the right people for these jobs and employing their services appropriately is among the practical skills most clearly associated with good leadership.

Headship can't be done alone. You need to surround yourself with the best people by developing those you have and appointing new ones. Make sure the people you have are doing the right jobs.

A good ruler will invariably choose competent companions who offer honest advice in response to specific questions and carry out the business of the state without regard for their private interests; such people therefore deserve the rewards of honour, wealth, and power that unshakably secure their devotion to the leader. The first opinion which one forms of a prince is by observing the men he has around him; and foolish servants show the foolishness of their prince in choosing them.

Surround yourself with excellent, not self-serving, people who advise you honestly and challenge you. Reward them.

Ineffective leaders, on the other hand, surround themselves with flatterers whose unwillingness to provide competent advice is a mark of their princes' inadequacy – don't surround yourself with yes men.

Acknowledging the possibilities for failure, the skilful ruler does better to act boldly than to try to calculate every possible eventuality – take calculated risks. The future is not fixed. You can help shape it by what you do.

Those emperors of Rome who succeeded had the difficulty of pleasing the people, the nobles and the army. Which three, being of opposing humours, they chose to satisfy the army, for if a prince cannot help being hated by some, he must avoid the hatred of the strongest – whom should you set out to work for? It's the children, stupid (and their parents).

Therefore, a wise prince ought to seek the honest council of only a few wise men, and afterwards form his own conclusions. Outside of these, he should listen to no one, and be steadfast in his resolutions. He who does otherwise is either overthrown by flatterers, or is so often changed in opinions that he falls into contempt – have your vision and direct all your efforts towards realising it.

A prince, therefore, ought to be a constant inquirer, and a patient listener, and should let his anger fall on those who have not told him the truth – never rest on your laurels.

Headship at times needs to combine the pursuit of high ideals through low cunning. You should never do anything illegal or dangerous, but you should be willing to challenge and subvert the status quo. If a particular piece of advice from the LA or government will take you further from your vision, find a way of not doing it. Remember that it is better to seek forgiveness than ask permission.

This is all about taking a risk. Often if you ask advice – of the LA, the DCSF, HR, whoever – their response will be circumscribed by rules and regulations. Not all will be relevant to your case; more often it is a case of their watching their backs. Unless it is likely to affect the safety of a child, it is usually worth taking a risk. Often it will work, sometimes it won't. You seek forgiveness when it doesn't.

Chapter 10 Lifelong learning for heads

You've achieved your headship, you may even have an NPQH, but the learning can't stop there.

1. Learning on the job – otherwise known as learning from experience or 'I wouldn't do it that way again.' Painful, occasionally slow, it has the benefit of being first-hand concrete experience.
2. Go on a course – your LA and your professional association almost certainly offer them and the NCSL run lots. Try to find out from colleagues what these are like before committing yourself. Remember, if it becomes clear in the middle of a training session that it is a waste of time, walk out politely.
3. Networking – learn from your peers. Your LA may provide you with a mentor when you become head. There may be cluster or wider headteacher meetings. Sometimes these can be tedious and seem irrelevant, but in a room of 20 heads there'll be hundreds of years of headship experience, some about doing the job badly, but some spot on. If there isn't one, set one up. You and some colleagues could start your own. Do learning walks in each other's schools, or meet for a drink and a chance to set the educational world to rights.
4. Take a master's in business studies if you really want to wind up traditionalists.
5. Set up a database of expertise. One head may have experience in dealing with capability, another with bereavement – enable everyone to share it and access support when they need it.
6. Volunteer for LA committees. This may be tedious on occasion, but it may be enlightening. You're giving something to the education community and gaining a chance to shape and influence policy and practice beyond your school.
7. Train to be a School Improvement Partner or an Ofsted inspector – learn how they operate. The quality of training at this level is usually very good.
8. Join the NCSL online learning community.

And finally ...

Anyone who was a student in the 1980s will be familiar with a poster featuring the poem 'Desiderata'. It adorned a thousand student walls. It was a bit hippyish but it brought a certain serenity and comfort to some. I leave you with my own version for headteachers.

Headteacher's desiderata

Go not placidly amidst the noise and haste, for you are the boss and you will get the blame.

All you need is love.

Listen to others, even the dull and the ignorant, yea because you too are dull and ignorant sometimes.

Beware the cupboard tidiers for they are avoiding doing anything of any real use.

A tidy desk is the mark of a scoundrel or a bore or a boring scoundrel.

Enjoy your achievements as well as your plans.

Strive for high ideals, but remember that their realisation sometimes requires low cunning.

Do not distress yourself with dark imaginings – or not often and never on a Friday at half past three.

If you start enjoying meetings, get your deputy to slap you hard. If you start enjoying the slap, it's time to retire.

You are only as good as the people you surround yourself with.

Barefoot, or shod in expensive Jimmy Choos, walk with serenity out of that useless INSET.

Surround yourself with excellence to keep the mundane and mediocre at bay.

It takes fewer muscles to smile than to frown, but those frown muscles need occasional exercise when someone cheeses you off.

One person nodding in agreement at a staff meeting is validation, two are cause for rejoicing and three means you've spiked their hedgerow infusion decaf with happy pills.

Meetings of education professionals will spin out for two hours what can be achieved in two minutes – so stop paying attention when the two minutes are up.

Children can spot a phoney at a hundred metres.

If a thing's worth doing it's sometimes worth doing with the minimum effort and time spent on it.

Each day, tell your good teachers how good they are.

Show your inadequate teachers how to improve. If they look the other way show them the door.

Everyone in school is a volunteer, often paid. If they don't like your school they are free to go elsewhere.

Bad times will pass.

Imagine your death bed – if you think your last words will be 'I don't regret a moment spent conscientiously implementing that patently useless government initiative', go ahead and spend your time doing just that.

The good times *will* roll – but only if you let them.